Ogham Inscriptions in Ireland, Wales, and Scotland

Samuel Ferguson

BIBLIOLIFE

OGHAM INSCRIPTIONS

IN

IRELAND, WALES, AND SCOTLAND

BY THE LATE

SIR SAMUEL FERGUSON

PRESIDENT OF THE ROYAL IRISH ACADEMY; DEPUTY KEEPER OF THE RECORDS OF IRELAND;
LL.D. DUBLIN AND EDINBURGH; ETC., ETC.

EDINBURGH: DAVID DOUGLAS
1887

PREFACE.

In the autumn of 1884, Sir Samuel Ferguson, President of the Royal Irish Academy, delivered in Edinburgh the Rhind Lectures on Archæology, and at the request of the committee he selected for his subject "Ogham Inscriptions." He had for many years taken a keen interest in this form of writing, which consists of notches of various lengths cut on the edge or arris of suitable stones, generally unhewn, and frequently standing pillars of striking dimensions. These are found in certain districts of Ireland, Wales, and Scotland, including the islands of Orkney and Shetland, and in a few instances in south-western England, and in the Isle of Man. The Ogham bears a certain resemblance to the Scandinavian Rune. Both seem designedly obscure, although in ancient Irish manuscripts a key to the interpretation of Ogham is given. In some cases, as in South Wales for instance, epigraphs in Roman characters occupy the face of the stone, while Ogham-writing on the edges has been found to contain an echo of the same. It will readily be understood that the value of these bi-lingual examples, as a test of correct rendering of the Ogham, is very great.

The stones are generally to be met with in remote and un-cultivated districts, not unfrequently in disused churchyards, reserved for the burial of unbaptized children and suicides. On land more valuable for agriculture they have been broken up, or removed for safety to the vicinity of the nearest church, or set up in private demesnes. In Ireland many of these in-scribed stones are found on the summits of lofty mountains or on lonely moors; they abound on the rugged storm-swept promontories which, on the south and west of the island, are washed by the Atlantic. Again, others are found on the ele-vated tracts of comparatively barren land which form the water-sheds of the Southern rivers and divide their basins, notably those of the Blackwater, Lee, and Bandon.

For many years it had been the habit of Sir Samuel Ferguson to spend his summer holiday in visiting these monuments. His time and energies for the rest of the year were devoted to his professional or official duties, but his annual vacation was consecrated to the pursuit of poetry, literature, or antiquities. The sedentary life of the city was then laid aside, and the long summer days were passed driving about the country, in search of these and kindred objects of interest. The rough accommodation and homely fare which these excursions often entailed, were not without their attraction for him; his genial nature was happy in simple intercourse with his fellow-man, while the varied beauties of the external world ever gave to him deep and keen delight. Year after year every nook and corner of Ireland and Wales was thus explored.

In his earlier expeditions, Sir Samuel had to content himself with rubbings and careful copies of the Ogham inscriptions, which were afterwards carried home and studied at leisure; but in these there were elements of uncertainty and error which made them far from satisfactory. On more than one occasion, finding the reading doubtful, Sir Samuel has taken the night train and started off from his home to the distant spot where the stone was to be found, in order to verify a single letter. Later he adopted a method of making paper casts, which obviated these uncertainties, and secured an entirely accurate *facsimile* of the stone with all its markings. The process is simple, and may be described for the benefit of others. The stone to be operated upon is first cleared of lichen and washed clean with water. Then a sheet of unsized paper (good thick blotting paper leaves nothing to be desired) is laid over the inscription, and slightly moistened with a sponge. A soft brush—an old hat brush is best—is then applied to the paper. It is patted gently till it sinks into every crevice and marking of the stone. Should the indentation be so deep as to break the surface of the paper, a fragment suitable in size must be torn off a fresh sheet, freed from any margin, applied to the broken surface, wetted, and duly patted with the brush until it becomes amalgamated with the pulp-like paper. Then a coat of paste must be lightly brushed over the entire surface of the paper covering the inscription, a second sheet of blotting paper laid on, and the process of slightly moistening and patting repeated. This must be permitted, as far as practicable, to dry upon the stone; hence the advisability of making the paper as little moist as possible. This cast, when dry, becomes as firm as cardboard, and can be easily lifted and removed. It retains every marking *in intaglio* and in relief, according as it is studied from the inside or the outside.

One day—typical of many others—at the close of a holiday spent by Sir Samuel Ferguson and his wife in exploring the antiquities of Kerry, Dunmore Head was visited. This is a noble mountain on the extreme western verge of the island, which, as well as its neighbour mountain, Brandon Head, bears on its summit a fine Ogham-inscribed pillar stone. A long drive from Dingle brought the little party to the base of the mountain. Here they dismounted and ascended on foot, while the driver led the horse over the grassy slopes as far as it was possible for a vehicle to travel. At the homestead of a farmer on the mountain side, a halt was called. With kindly grace both horse and man were here made welcome to a rest, while the sons of the house shouldered the box which contained the preparations for cast-taking, and led the way up the steep precipitous path, over crags and boulders, until the summit was gained. The prospect which lay before the eye was of a beauty never to be forgotten. The Blasket Islands lay below, fringed with the white foam of Atlantic waves—the broad, boundless, heaving floor of ocean stretching beyond, unbroken by any land nearer than America. On one of the bold headlands of the Dingle Peninsula, not far distant, stood Smerwick Fort, where the hapless Spanish garrison, hemmed in by the overwhelming forces of Queen Elizabeth's Deputy, Lord Grey,* was obliged to capitulate, in the summer of 1580, only to meet in cold blood their wretched fate. Looking inland from Dunmore lay the picturesque region of

---

* Amongst Lord Grey's troops were many names dear to fame—Sir Walter Raleigh, Edmund Spenser, &c.

Corkaguiny, studded with those mysterious monuments of a
remote past which had attracted Sir Samuel Ferguson hither,
and amongst which he had spent some previous weeks.*

After some diligent work a fine cast of the pillar-stone on
Dunmore Head was taken, but before it was yet dry enough to
remove, a furious gale arose, accompanied by torrents of rain.
The stone was quickly enveloped in waterproof and great
coat, whilst their owners. denuded of them, and regardless of
the storm, stood close, so as still further to protect the precious
cast. By and by the storm abated, but not until the day
was already far spent, and the deepening shadows threatened
to benight the party in their dangerous position on the wild
mountain. Cautiously the cast was loosened—the protecting
waterproof still held over it,—but it was moist and pulpy.
At last, at the most critical moment, when about to be transferred to the box, a sudden gust of wind got under, and in an
instant it was carried aloft. The toilers stood dismayed,
watching its gyrations in upper air until the precious thing,
torn to pieces, was whirled into the Atlantic! Weary, wet,
and disappointed, they descended the mountain to the house,
where horse and car were waiting; here the travellers found
a hospitable meal of tea and eggs prepared, for which their
kindly hosts would receive no payment; warmed and fed
they continued their way, returning on the following day,
when, under bright sun and fair skies, a wholly successful
cast of the stone was made, and carried off in safety.

The spoils of a summer holiday were the material for a
winter's work. During the last months of Sir Samuel's life,
when health had given way, and he was no longer able
to move about as of old, he would have the casts brought to
his bedside, and with feeble hands he would turn and examine
them, and endeavour to unravel their true significance. As
long as he could hold a pen, he continued to add to and
correct the proofs of these Lectures. Those on Irish Oghams
were revised by him, but the chapters on Welsh and Scottish
inscribed-stones had not been fully annotated when he died.

* This group contains the singular Christian edifice of Gallerus. Also a beautiful
church probably erected in the twelfth century, containing exquisite decorative ornament. This ruined church of Kilmalkedar is a fine example of the Irish Romanesque

Since his death, three friends whom he loved and esteemed in life have been good enough to read the sheets of these Lectures—Dr. Ingram, LL.D., Vice-President of the Royal Irish Academy, S.F.T.C.D.; Dr. Anderson, Keeper of the National Museum of the Antiquaries of Scotland; and, as regards two chapters, Dr. Whitley Stokes, D.C.L. To these gentlemen, friends and scholars, the warmest thanks are due, and are here tendered.

Sir Samuel Ferguson had not personally examined the monuments of Scotland. He knew them only from rubbings and casts made by others. The latter portion of this book must, therefore, be deemed comparatively imperfect. Indeed he would himself have been the first to acknowledge the tentative character of the work, and probably have considered that the data are as yet too limited to justify scholars in formulating absolute conclusions. He claims only the "credit of having supplied their researches with approximately authentic data in the texts presented." He might justly have laid claim to more than this, for he made with his own hands casts of nearly all the Oghams in Ireland, England, and Wales. One hundred and sixty-three of these casts have been photographed under his superintendence for the Royal Irish Academy, and of these, some twenty-one have already been published in the 27th volume of their Transactions. Whenever the Academy completes the series, scholars will have before them, for reference, indisputable *facsimiles* of these Ogham-inscribed stones as they now exist.

No one could be more candid, modest, or free from dogmatism than was Sir Samuel Ferguson. In all his instincts he was disinterested, true, generous, and noble. He died as he had lived, revered and beloved, and enjoying in full measure that which should accompany old age — "Honour, love, obedience, troops of friends."

M. C. F.

20 North Great George's-street, Dublin,
December, 1886.

CONTENTS.

CHAPTER I

CHAPTER II.

CHAPTER III.

CHAPTER IV.

CHAPTER I.

Ogham Inscriptions in Great Britain and Ireland—Those verified from casts represented in Roman capital letters ; those less certain, in Italic—The Ogham of the
same family with the Runic alphabet—According to the Irish tradition introduced
from Northern Europe by the Tuatha de Danaan colonists—Difficulties in reading
these Inscriptions—Labours of Petrie, O'Donovan, Windele, Brash, Horgan,
Graves, Hitchcock, Du Noyer, Haigh, Atkinson, Rhys—Necessity of authentic
texts—Paper casts easily photographed—The main question dealt with, Whether
the Ogham is of Pagan or Christian origin ? &c.

1. THE only Celtic Monumental Inscriptions in these islands,
which can at the present day be said to need further elucidation, are those conceived in the Ogham form of writing. Ogham inscrip-
Further study and inquiry may contribute some additions and tions
corrections, but, that anything substantial remains to be done
for a satisfactory general acquaintance with Scottish, Welsh, or
Irish inscriptional antiquities of the ordinary alphabetic kind,
seems unlikely. We shall, therefore, be concerned in the
present inquiry with the Ogham variety, and such topics as
legitimately associate themselves with it. To present perfect
pictures of Ogham inscriptions would require the reproduction of photographs taken from casts of the originals. A from casts
fasciculus of twenty-five such reproductions has been printed
by the Royal Irish Academy as part of its 27th volume of
Transactions, not yet published. Instead of these costly illustrations, the readers of the present work will, I hope, be content
with the reproduction in Roman print of those examples represented in
which I can personally vouch for from casts mostly in my Roman print;
possession. In the primary transliteration of these, the Roman
capital will be employed for such characters as are certain,
the Italicised capital for such as are presumable from remaining indications, and the Roman minuscule where the indications have wholly disappeared, and the *lacunœ* are filled up
hypothetically. Where alternative powers have to be represented, the several letters will be arranged vertically, the

B

not from casts, in Italic.

more probable above. For such examples as I cannot so vouch, Italicised minuscules will be employed.

2. Monuments so inscribed exist to the number of nearly two hundred in Ireland. There are eighteen in Wales, two in South England, at least six on the mainland of Scotland, and four in the Orkney and Shetland Islands. The general key to the reading has been traditionally preserved in Ireland; and could be re-constructed, if necessary, from the Roman epigraphs which accompany and echo the Oghams on the biliteral monuments of Wales. The subjects of the texts are almost exclusively proper names connected by the word *Maqi*, accepted as meaning "son of." Although a series of proper names is not calculated to excite much interest in the abstract, there are historical and palæographic considerations which give these monuments a claim on the attention of British archæologists not much inferior to that of the Rune for Scandinavian scholars.

Key preserved.

3. The Ogham is to this extent of the same family with the Rune, that the characteristic of both kinds of writing is the employment of straight strokes easily carved on wood or stone for forming the alphabetic letters. The original Runic alphabet, however, is not, like the Ogham, of a cryptic nature; but it is the foundation on which the cryptic Tree-Runes, having several points of resemblance to the Ogham, are founded. Rune, in the northern languages as well as in the Celtic, signifies something secret, but the Futhorc or Scandinavian alphabet cannot be said to be more secret or mysterious than any other, and, if it bore the name of Rune in its original state, it probably was because alphabetic writing of any kind was deemed a mystery by the northern populations to whom it was first imparted, or by those amongst whom it may have been first invented. The Tree-Rune, however, founded on it, is a designedly secret and highly artificial kind of writing. The Futhorc (so called from commencing with F, U, Th, O, R, C) consists of sixteen letters, represented, in the Tree-Rune, by an equal number of characters formed in this way. The Futhorc is arranged in three divisions—the first of six letters, as above; the second of five, H, N, I, A, S; and the third of five, T, B, L, M, Y. These divisions or categories are known

Related to the Rune.

Tree-Rune

formed on Futhorc alphabet.

as Frey's *Aett* (sort or kind), Hagel's *Aett*, and Tyr's *Aett*. The corresponding cryptic characters are conceived in the form of trees or upright stems with branches. The branches issuing from the side of the stem to the spectator's left, which may be called the index side, indicate the number of the *Aett* or division of the Futhorc in which the letter is found; those issuing from the opposite side, indicate the number of the letter in its division, as first to sixth in the first *Aett*, and first to fifth in the two others. As, if it were required to express the syllable MAN in Tree-Runes, M would be represented by a stem having three branches to the spectator's left, to indicate the third category, and four branches to the right, because in that category M stands fourth. A would have two branches on the one side and four on the other, as indicating the second category, and fourth place in it; and N, in like manner, would be shown to be second of the second, thus—

Or, cross-lines being drawn, branches may be shown issuing to the right from one extremity and to the left from the other, each bar of the cross thus serving for a separate Runic letter,

and as many crosses as there are pairs of letters in the legend may be engraved lattice-wise on the face of the monument; or, yet a third way, on the worm-band or ribbon formed by the outline of the snake which generally enters into the ornamentation of a Norse sculptural monument, digits may be shown,

some of which cross the half and some the whole of its width, the former indicating the *Aett,* and the latter the sub-number in the *Aett* of the letter so represented.

4. In the Ogham, a process of much the same kind seems to have been adopted, not on the foundation of the Futhorc, but of another alphabet differing from the Futhorc both in the names, numbers, and sequences of its letters. This is the Irish *Bethluisnion*—an alphabet designated altogether by names of trees, but represented, in its Oghamic equivalents, by straight strokes, the significance of which depends primarily on a division of the *Bethluisnion* into like categories as the Futhorc, with this difference, that, in preparing the *Bethluisnion* for its relations with these equivalents, it is divided into four categories of five each, thus—B, L, F S, N; H, D, T, C, Q; M, G, NG, ST, R; A, O, U, E, I,—which divisions, also, as in the Futhorc, have their names of the ' B ' *aicme* (kind or following), the ' H ' *aicme*, the ' M ' *aicme*, and the ' A ' *aicme*. So far the resemblances are obvious. In the next step, in which, instead of the several stems of the Tree-Runes, one common stem line is provided for all the characters, the resemblance is still discernible; and in the ultimate arrangement, by which the straight strokes or digits of the Ogham are given their alphabetic values by reference to this stem line, the parallelism, although not so obvious, still exists. In the Ogham, the letters of each *aicme* are represented by a set of strokes beginning with a single digit, and increasing in progressive order from one to five; and according as these digits and groups of digits are arranged under, over, across, or on the stem line, they represent the letters of the first, second, third, and fourth *aicmes* respectively, on the plan of one digit for the first letter, two for the second, and so on to five digits for the fifth letter of each *aicme*; thus—

Here we see the same guiding principles of numerical and local relation determining the values both of the Ogham and of the Tree-Rune, although with differences in their application which make it difficult, notwithstanding the other points of resemblance, to say that either system is derived from the other, although both might well be thought to have originated in some older common parentage. If either is to be deemed a derivative, it is, most probably, the Tree-Rune, of which, I believe, no examples have been found older than those of Mæshow, belonging to the period of the Jerusalem pilgrimages.

5. But the Irish *Bethluisnion* does not exist, as the Futhorc does, in the form of a lettered original alphabet. None but Roman and Ogham letters have, as yet, been found on the Celtic monuments of these islands. The *Bethluisnion* is only a vocabulary of letter-names adaptable to the letter-signs either of the Roman alphabet or of the fuller and, it is thought, the older form of the Futhorc. If the Futhorc and Tree-Rune be excluded, we should conclude that the Ogham has been founded on the Roman alphabet, re-named and marshalled into the *Bethluisnion* sequence. The account, however, which the Irish themselves give of it is, that it was brought in by the early half-mythical colony of the Tuatha de Danaan, whom they bring from the northern parts of the world through Scotland. ·

6. There is one feature in the Ogham which seems to establish that its framers were of the Latin rather than the Teutonic branch of the European family. The 'h' *aicme* (h, d, t, c, q) is apparently an anagram drawn from the initial letters of the cardinal numbers, one, two, three, four, five—that is, in insular Celtic speech, *h'œn, da, tri, cathar, cuig.* Whether it was an original lost Irish alphabet, a Futhorc of the longer sort, or the Latin alphabet of the Romans that formed the foundation for the Ogham, it must be recognised that the people who adjusted it to its fourfold division and locative values in the Oghamic system did not express their numerals " four" or "five" with an initial *p*, as Teutonic or Cymric speakers probably would have done. A fifth division of five further signs for the shorter expression of the diphthongs has been added, at a later date. It is called the *Forfeada* or " over-trees," as being supplementary, and does not enter into the older examples.

The first and third of these are the only ones I have found in lapidary use.

7. If derived from the Rune, its framers have not

Its disadvan-
tages as com-
pared with the
Rune,

succeeded in improving on the original, either in perspicuous-
ness or fitness for monumental use. The Ogham is very much
more cumbrous than the Futhorc, and, notwithstanding the
apparent simplicity of its arrangement, has an inherent element
of uncertainty, unknown. I believe, in any other alphabet.
The distinctive shapes of the letters of the Futhorc, and the
slope of the Tree-Rune branches, always assure us against
reading the letter-band upside down, or, in the Futhorc,
in an order reverse to that intended by the carver. But the

uncertainty
owing to re-
versible values,

nature of the Ogham is such, that a digit or group of digits
which, looked at from one side, appears below the line, will
appear above it, and express a different letter, if looked at from
the other; and that, unless there be some sign, as in old Ogham
there never is, to indicate from which end of the legend the
reading is to commence, a trial reading must be made from each
end as well as each side. For example, in the syllable *man*,

it is obvious that the legend will read *man*, *nam*, *maq*, or *qam*,
according as it is regarded from below or above, or read from
either end. This difficulty, of course, disappears where a known
group of letters catches the eye and rectifies the situation, but
in the absence of such catch-words error often arises.

8. The reading which generally gives the right transliteration proceeds from left to right ; but this implies that the
legend is first put in readable position ; for there might
equally well be a reading from left to right from the other end,
if the reader changed his place to the opposite side. These
confusions, however, are lessened by the practice of the early
Irish Ogham carvers of utilising the continuous edges or arrises
of standing stones, or of stones to be placed in a standing
position, for their common stem-lines. In such situations an
Ogham legend generally begins from below on that angle of
the stone to the left hand of the spectator regarding it from
the front; but if carried over the head of the stone and down
the opposite angle, it will sometimes be uncertain whether the

to shift of
reader's posi-
tion,

carver intended his reader to retain his position or to shift it
with the shifting stem-line, and in this way a true and valuable

reading in its beginning may be discredited by an unintelligible ending. The Mount Brandon inscription, in the same district of Kerry, which gives along the northern arris of its west face the word *Cruimthir*, the old Irish equivalent of Presbyter—in the Oghamic form *Qrrimitir*,—where carried over the head of the stone and returned down the southern arris seems to make this Presbyter the son of *Somogaq*—a name unlike anything likely to be authentic, but which, as pointed out by the Bishop of Limerick, is really the well-known name *Comogan* in the altered adjustment due to a change of the reader's position. Thus, though an Ogham digit or group of digits has nothing *per se* to show which is top or which bottom, the right position and sequences of such a legend can generally, after a little experience, be ascertained.

9. An example of a legend conceived throughout in retrograde sequence is afforded by a very fine Ogham pillar-stone now in the Lapidary Museum of the Royal Irish Academy. It is one of a group of similar monuments dug up from a cave at Monataggart, in the parish of Donoughmore, in the northern to retrograde part of East Cork. Read upward from below, with its inscribed sequence, angle facing the spectator's left, it yields the impracticable sequence—

tenrenmonoigduqdeggef,

but, on being read from the opposite side of the arris with inverse values, it gives the legend—

feqreq moqoi glunlegget,

being in commemoration of some Fiachra (genitive Feqreq), to whom the designations Mocoi and Glunlegget, the latter probably signifying the "Kneeler," seem to be ascribed; and so of several other retroverse and inverted readings of the same kind.

10. Again, where the Rune-Smith could fall into no confusion of letter-forms unless he desired to exhibit a deliberate ligature or *siglum* where one character should have the force of several letters, the Ogham carver, in engraving some of his groups, had to encounter the difficulty of accurate spacing, lest, in writing, let us say, two B's or two D's or two M's, he should not make them so close as to appear *l*, *c*, or *g*, respectively; as, for example, in the Lunnasting Ogham in the Museum of the Society of Antiquaries of Scotland, it is doubtful whether the reading should be *agofest* or *ammofest*; owing to the indecision of the carver in the spacing of these two stem crossing digits which make *mm* or *g* according to the greater or less distance between them. This source of error is even more troublesome in long vocalic groups, where points which make several vowels succeed one another, without distinctions of space. A fine Ogham pillar from Kerry, now in the Museum of Trinity College, Dublin, exemplifies this and another source of ambiguity in Ogham writing originating in the carelessness or caprice of the scribe. The arrises of the pillar are rounded, and the value of the characters depends on their relation to the general line of convexity. Two groups, each of seven equally-spaced digits, occur in the text, and some others are so ambiguously placed in relation to the medial ridge as to leave it doubtful whether we are to read the diphthongs *oi*, *io*, *eu*, or in some other of the various combinations of which they are capable; and whether, having regard to the relations of the other groups to the ridge, we are to read them *eedduini* or *seddacini*.

11. But the practice of using the natural stem line of the arris has led to even greater difficulties of decipherment than these inherent uncertainties of the system. In every cubical block it is the arris that first gets chipped and abraded. In blocks of laminated rock the adjacent faces on either side of the line disintegrate unequally, and one half of a stem-crossing digit may sometimes disappear, while the other half is plainly visible; as in the first proposed example now represented vertically as it would appear on the arris of an upright pillar—

Here the loss of the half-digit to the left of, or above, the line, would leave the letters forming *ban*,—of the half-digit to the right, or below the line, those forming *han*. Or, weathering and erosion may wholly obliterate a digit, and in many such cases call into existence a new letter, as, if one digit be taken from the concluding N, the remainder makes S, and one from S makes F, and one from F leaves L. There exists a very grand and imposing block of conglomerate at Ballyquin, near Carrick-on-Suir, in the County of Waterford, which appears to have once borne, in largely-proportioned shallow digits, the legend—*Catabar moqo Firiquorr*(b). But the final groups are only visible in a favourable light, and some of the digits retain their outlines more distinctly about the middle point of their length, and so might in some lights and to some eyes appear as vowels. The terminal group has so come to be read as if Cathbar were the son of *Firiqongo*, where the name commemorated is that of *Cathbar* the son of *Fercorb*. The cross fractures, again, to which such monuments are subject, may take away some digits of a group and leave others. As, at Templemanahan, a terminal fracture at the top of the stone has left three over-line digits

of what the context shows were probably four; and, at Ardmore, three under-line digits in a like predicament,

converting the presumptive *c* into *t* in the one instance and *s* into *f* in the other.

12. With so many causes of uncertainty, inherent and external, it is not surprising that scholars fifty years ago looked on Oghamic investigation as an unpromising employment. Sir James Ware and Mr. Astle had made public the fact that such an alphabet existed, and that Irish manuscripts of respectable antiquity professed to give examples of several varieties of it, and to furnish the keys. Lhuyd, the father of Cambro-British archæology, had seen the Ogham-inscribed stone of *Bruscos* on the strand of Trabeg Creek, near Dingle Harbour, in Kerry.

Petrie had made known the general appearance of such a monument by his drawing of the Ogham-inscribed pillar-stone at St. Manchan's, in the same neighbourhood ; but he did not at that time regard such an inscription as true alphabetic writing, and attempted no transliteration of the digits he had drawn. Excellent and conscientious draftsman though he was, he had indeed mis-copied not less than five out of the twenty-four letter-equivalents made up of seventy-eight digits of which the legend consists ; and, had he essayed the transliteration, would have elicited little that could be called articulate and nothing intelligible. His doubts were shared by O'Donovan, whose scepticism was the more weighty because, of all our Irish scholars, he was best acquainted with what bardic writers had said in their frequent allusions to Ogham as a known system of alphabetic writing, and with the numerous keys and paradigms which the mediæval grammarians professed to give of it.

But at this time O'Donovan had not had the experience which shortly after befell him, when, in his enquiry after material for the then projected Ordnance Survey Memoir of Ireland, he found himself under the Ogham-inscribed roofing-stones of the Cave of Dunloe, and had to acknowledge that he stood in the presence of a long past age speaking to us by intelligible, articulate signs. Petrie, too, before his death, would no doubt have wished that passage of his essay expunged, in which he challenged the Munster Antiquaries to show that the inscription in this character preserved in the Cathedral at Ardmore, and which they thought Druidical, was " literary writing of any

kind." These Munster Antiquaries were men of moderate scholastic acquirements, but sincere and very ardent explorers of the antiquities of their country. The leading spirit amongst

them was the late Mr. John Windele, of the City of Cork, a man of great natural ability, and of that contagious genius which attracts, and propagates itself in the minds of others. They had already ascertained the existence of a considerable number of Ogham-inscribed monuments in the counties of Cork, Waterford, and Kerry. Mr. Windele himself had visited and copied most of the legends, among the rest that at Bally-quin, which he made *Catabar moco festiqonga.* His transcripts of the numerous other texts from time to time copied by him are less inaccurate than probably most other draftsmen at that period of the inquiry could have produced, but are, in every case which I have seen, more or less imperfect; and, as if conscious of this defect, although well acquainted with the key, he never himself professed to have read or even transliterated any of them. Key known popularly.

13. The key was indeed known to many of the old Irish-speaking people of the country. It had been transmitted in many treatises. Of these the principal is that contained in the Book of Ballymote, a late fourteenth-century compilation. Besides the regular Ogham alphabet, it professes to give about fifty derivative variations, but these are, in great part, illusory, the differences consisting only in the letter-names, or in the use of particular objects instead of the regular digits. The remainder are produced by duplications, transpositions, and inversions—some sufficiently transparent and even puerile, others more difficult: as, for example, *Ogham comesgda*, the confused or drunken Ogham, where the second letter of one *aicme* is used for the first letter of another; and *Ogham rinn fri derca*, where the *aicmes* are not only inverted, but interchanged. Three only of these curious exercises of ingenuity appear to be relevant to the present inquiry. In one, the *Run Ogham na Fian*, the digits of what, at first sight, appear distinct over- and under-line groups not exceeding three in number, are discontinuously apposited so as to overlap, and, by combination, to serve the purpose of the normal five digits, and, where vowels are indicated, as they generally are in what I shall call Scholastic Ogham, by stem-crossing digits, the same artifice appears applicable. In another, the *Nathair im ceann*, or "head-coiled snake," an inverted name is written before the same name written direct, and the legend reads outward from the centre to either end, yielding the same name (here *Cellac*) both ways; Key in Book of Ballymote with variations. Examples.

and in the other, the *Gleselga*, "the chase-feat," the first half of one name is written before the first half of another; then the second halves in like order, as—

Feth : Seg : nat : nat.
Fethnat, Segnat.

As succeeding scribes got farther from original examples, their inventions became more idle and conceited, comprising *Naomh Ogham*, where the letters have the names of saints, as Brendan, Laisren, Fintan, &c. ; *Dan Ogham*, where they are called after branches of knowledge, as if we, in English, should say for B, Biology, for L, Logics, and so on; *Biad Ogham*, after articles of diet, as Bacon, Lamb, Fowl, &c., and other such ineptitudes for which the later Irish penmen had a singularly childish partiality.   All these variations, however, are grounded on the original Ogham alphabet, of which the tradition of the country never lost sight.   Although they took no notice or care of the monuments, the old people preserved the key to the cypher, and had it committed to English country verse long before the days of Lhuyd and Astle.

For B one stroke at your right hand,
And L doth always two demand.
For F draw three; for S make four;
When you want N, you add one more,

and so on through the alphabet in ill-rhymed but intelligible lines.   Mr. Windele relates an instance of its use in our own times which is worth preserving :—

"The oddest use I have seen made of this letter was by a man named Collins, living at Duneen, near the old Head of Kinsale. This man had a favourite walking-stick of goodly size, which he coloured black, and on it painted with a white oil-colour a long Irish poem on the Zodiac in the Ogham character. This stick is now in my possession, and is a very striking instance of a patient labour of love. The same person put his name in similar characters on his cart, [and was summoned] before the Magistrates at Petty Sessions. On the evidence, however, of the Rev. Dan. O'Sullivan, now P.P. of Inniskeen, a most competent witness on all subjects pertaining to such literature, Collins was discharged, but recommended by the magistrates to append on his cart shaft a translation."—(Windele MSS., R.I.A., iii., 148 b.)

Windele's monument.

14. Yet such was Windele's love of the subject, as much I imagine for its mystery as for its significance, that, although a pious and orthodox member of the Roman Catholic Church, he

chose for the headstone of his own grave a fine Ogham-inscribed
monolith bearing at top a deeply-incised Maltese cross, which
doubtless he believed had been superadded by a Christian
hand to some Pagan memento of religion or philosophy conveyed by the Ogham. Amongst his younger associates was
the late Mr. Richard Rolt Brash, of the City of Cork, architect, Brash.
a man of excellent powers of observation combined with an
acute judgment and warm enthusiasm, who, after Windele's
death, continued to prosecute the Oghamic inquiry with equal
industry, but with greatly enlarged resources in material as well
as in scholastic aids, and who, addressing himself to a very
much wider circle, has made a name which will long survive in
connection with this kind of learning. Another of Windele's
associates was the late Rev. Mathew Horgan, Parish Priest of Horgan.
Blarney, who, there seems no doubt, recognised the often-
recurring group

as the equivalent of *Maqi*, 'son of,' at an early period in their
researches. A characteristic etching of this genial ecclesiastic
among the Windele papers now at the Royal Irish Academy
is, I believe, from the pen of the painter Maclise, also one of Maclise.
the circle drawn together by the winning force of Windele's
character.

15. It is impossible not to extend a large amount of sympathy
to these eager South Irish antiquaries. Fully persuaded of the Characteristics
Pagan origin of the Round Towers, and of an age of literary of their school.
culture before the introduction of Christianity, they regarded
their Oghamic discoveries as so many Orphic fragments from
which primæval learning would, sooner or later, in some
measure, be reconstructed; and contested, with an ardour far
too hot, every opinion which did not tend to advance their
views and aspirations. This heat belonged to their period and
local tone of society; and, if it must now be allowed to have been
unsuitable for the search after historical truth, we may also
make some allowance for the excesses of an ardour which had
nothing dishonest or uncandid in it. But there is no pursuit in
which more room should exist for distrust of one's own obser-

vation or gentleness in dissenting from the observations of others, than this research in a field where so many accidents of light and position conduce to varieties of impression on different eyes, and to conflicts of statement among eye-witnesses.

> " 'Tis green, 'tis green, sir, I assure you."
> " Green ? " cries the other in a fury ;
> " Why, sir, d'ye think I've lost my eyes ? "—

The Southern school had, indeed, no toleration for anyone who would not see with their eyes both sensibly and in the way of ratiocination; and much of the efficiency which, in such a pursuit, flows from co-operation and mutual encouragement, has been lost to Oghamic research in Ireland in consequence.

16. While the Southern antiquaries were adding to the number of their discoveries, but not advancing in the use of accurate transcripts or reliable inductions, the Rev. Dr. Charles Graves (afterwards President of the Royal Irish Academy, now Bishop of Limerick) subjected the Ogham texts, so far as he could be assured of them, to the process which may be termed the cypher-test, assuming them to be written in the Irish of our oldest manuscripts. The proportionate percentage of each letter in the known text identifies the corresponding letter in the cypher. On this principle it appeared that the traditional key was in substantial accordance with the theoretic values of the letters so deduced, and Dr. Graves entered on further Oghamic inquiry with the assurance that he proceeded on firm ground. Shortly afterwards he was rewarded by the discovery of the biliteral monument at St. Dogmael's, in Wales, where the *Sagramni fili Cunotami* of the Latin is echoed by the Oghamic *Sagrani Maqi Cunatami*, putting the equivalence of Maqi to ' son of ' out of the way of doubt or question. Speedily other discoveries followed. It was ascertained that the Scottish Newton Stone, besides its seemingly Romanesque epigraph, bore a long Ogham legend, and that other Ogham inscriptions existed both in Wales and Scotland. One from Bressay, in the mainland of Shetland, was submitted to Dr. Graves, who found that the language was Norse, and that it seemed to commemorate a daughter and grandson of a known Scandinavian personage of the ninth century.

Graves

tests the key.

17. Considerable collections of Ogham transcripts had now accumulated at the Royal Irish Academy. Mr. Richard Hitch- Hitchcock. cock had sent up numerous copies, distinguished by care and substantial accuracy. He observed that upwards of thirty such monuments in Kerry and West Cork were marked with the sign of the cross. The Munster antiquaries, however, maintained that these crosses formed no part of the original design, but were the additions of Christian zealots who took this method of sanctifying Pagan remains; and, as often as cross-signed monu- Cross-signed ments bearing Ogham legends have since been discovered, have Ogham monu- ments. adhered with the utmost tenacity to this opinion, for which neither evidence nor the least presumption of probability exists. Mr. George Du Noyer also presented the Academy with several Du Noyer. volumes of admirably-executed drawings of various objects of antiquity throughout the country, including many transcripts of Ogham legends. Although a very accomplished draftsman, his texts are not to be relied on. He has a fine drawing of the Ballyquin monolith, but makes its legend *Catabar moco festiquar.*

18. Frequent communications now began to be made to the Royal Irish Academy, in some of which Bishop Graves contri- Graves's buted valuable results of his views on particular legends and essays. on the general subject. It was understood that he had for some time been engaged on a larger treatise, in which all the Irish tracts on Ogham writing would be discussed; but that expectation has not yet been fulfilled, although he still continues from time to time to enrich the Publications of the Academy with short, but singularly curious and elegant treatises on various branches of the subject.

19. The late Rev. Daniel Haigh, of Erdington, near Birming- Haigh ham, had applied himself with great learning and assiduity to British and old English antiquities, historical and monumental. He analysed (Proc., R. I. Academy) whatever Irish Ogham his essay. texts were accessible to him in 1876, and compared them critically with the Oghams and Brito-Roman epigraphs of Wales and South England. The conclusion which appears to have impressed itself on his mind was in favour of their very high antiquity, extending back through the early Christian into the Pagan period. His death has been a sensible loss to early

English literature, which he had enriched from Norse and Anglo-Saxon sources, and possibly, if he had lived, would have further illustrated from our little-used Irish material.

20. Brash, also, I grieve to say, is no longer with us. On his death, it appeared that he had devoted the later years of his life to the compilation of a considerable work on the general subject of Ogham inscriptions. His papers were put into the hands of Mr. G. M. Atkinson, of the Department of Science and Art, and, under his editorship, in 1879, appeared in a handsome and indeed a highly-interesting quarto volume, entitled " The Ogham-inscribed Monuments of the Gaedil in the British Islands."

21. Mr. Brash was a good draftsman, and his copious illustrations have been supplemented by Mr. Atkinson in several *facsimiles* and drawings, most of which are of remarkable fidelity. The work is written in accordance with the views of the Munster school. I am obliged to withhold my assent from many of the readings, and, I may say, from almost all the conclusions. It contains, however, much curious matter on collateral subjects, and in the further course of these investigations I shall thankfully make use of information drawn from it.

22. Another impulse to the inquiry has been given by the foundation, at Oxford, of a Professorship of Celtic. Professor Rhys, who fills that chair, besides being a scientific and general philologist, takes a particular interest in the old language and lapidary writing both of Wales and Ireland, and has travelled through both countries in search especially of Ogham inscriptions, on which he has already given us much valuable information and many helps to study in his published Lectures.

23. It would be premature, and, indeed, arrogant to pretend that any definite analysis of Ogham texts can be made in the present state of our knowledge. The only way in which the subject can be presented is as inviting to induction rather than as expounding inductive results. The whole of the material, so far as it can be authentically procured, must first be passed in review; and, from what has been seen of the extraordinary liability of these texts to errors of transcription, it is obvious that some kind of automatic reproduction of the objects themselves ought to be before us, if we

Atkinson.

Brash's conclusions not accepted.

Rhys

Lectures.

Investigation still tentative.

would be assured that our labour shall not be lost in the pursuit of phantoms, where the mistake of a digit or a notch may have altered the whole basis of our reasoning, and turned what ought to be fruitful investigation into mere illusion and reverie.

24. Such reproductions can be attained without the labour of transporting heavy masses of plaster of Paris, by means of Paper casts. This kind of cast has the advantage that it can *Paper casts.* be conveniently held in the hand and presented to the light in varying degrees of incidence—an important means of getting at the traces of worn inscriptions of all kinds. The Paper cast has the further advantage of pliability, so that an inscription extending to two surfaces which could not be seen on one plane reflected from a solid model, can easily be exposed on the flat to the photographer's lens. I have, therefore, from time to time procured Paper casts of most of the Oghams I shall refer to.

25. True texts being secured, the next requisite towards getting at the meaning is a right transliteration. There *Transliteration* being no word-divisions, save in a few exceptional cases, the *verbatim,* if I may so say, depends in a large degree on the knowledge and sagacity of the reader. I can here no longer speak with the same confidence. In what I shall propose in the way of reducing transliterations to words, and in giving to these words their English equivalents, I by no means claim for myself the same degree of certainty as in *liable to errors.* the assignment of the continuous values. If, hereafter, laws, grammatical or constructional, should appear to be legitimately deduced—and the probability of a large addition to the present material gives reasonable hope that such laws may yet be established,—a tone of authority may become justifiable; but at present the study is exploratory rather than demonstrative; and he who speaks with most modesty is the more likely to obtain an intelligent hearing from men of judgment.

26. The main questions agitated are : Whether the Ogham *Questions* is of Pagan or Christian origin ; Whether, if of Pagan origin, any *dealt with.* of the monuments are Christian ; Whether the Welsh imparted it to the Irish, or *vice versâ* ; and, Whether its forms belong to a vernacular or to an artificialised and technical language. Minor questions relate to the meaning of particular phrases or formulas which, from the frequency of their occurrence, seem to be removed from the category of proper names. I shall not be able definitively to clear up the meaning either of *Maqi mucoi* or of *Maqi decedda*; and I shall have to leave the question of Irish or British, as well as of Pagan or Christian origin, dependent on the question of language, which I do not profess to solve. I shall often have to say "perhaps," and often present alternative conclusions. These my readers will have to judge of for themselves; not that I shall withhold the expression of any opinion I may think myself capable of forming; but because my judgment in such cases will be of little more weight than that of any intelligent bystander. I shall be able, however, I think, to show reasonable grounds for believing that the bulk, if not all, of our Ogham monuments are Christian; that some of them represent, perhaps, as old a Christianity as has ever been claimed for the Church in either island; and that the "*Scoti in Christo credentes*," to whom Palladius was sent by Pope Celestine in the fifth century, were, especially in the south of Ireland, a more numerous and better organised community than has generally been

Conclusions drawn.

supposed. I shall, I think, bring Irish Pagan and British Christian monumental usage into actual contact in Wales; and contribute something towards the further elucidation, as Christian monuments, of the Sculptured Stones of Scotland. The bulk of the material, however, lying here, it is proposed to proceed, first, with a survey of the Ogham-inscribed monuments of Ireland.

CHAPTER II.

27. A SURVEY of the Ogham-inscribed monuments of Ireland KERRY may be conveniently commenced in the district where they (Corkaguiny). first attracted learned attention, that is, the Barony of Corka-guiny, in the County of Kerry. It is conterminous with the Peninsula of long peninsula which, reaching out more than thirty miles Corkaguiny. westward into the Atlantic, separates the Bay of Tralee on the north from the Bay of Dingle on the south. At the point where it juts from the mainland rises the lofty mountain group of Slieve Mish, overlooking the town of Tralee to the north. A prolongation of the Slieve Mish group, lower, but more varied in outline, runs along the medial line of the peninsula through about two-thirds of its length, and there, turning northward, unites itself with the outlying mass of Mount Brandon, which rises over the sea at the northern side. Dingle, situated on a creek on the southern side of the peninsula, in the more open country lying westward of these mountains, was formerly approached from Tralee by a highroad crossing the ridge which connects Brandon with the mountain chain first mentioned. The Tralee road now avoids this difficult pass by being carried obliquely through a depression in the medial mountain chain debouching at Annascaul on the southern line of coast road which leads to Dingle from Castlemaine and Killarney. Entering the district by this avenue, as from

KERRY
(Corkaguiny).

Castlemaine, Oghamic sites and monuments may be observed numerous on either hand as we proceed westwards.

28. After passing the ravine which separates Slieve Mish—with its ruined barbaric fortress of Cahir Conree on its western extremity,—from the lower eminences, we enter the parish of Ballinvoher, a rough, lonely country, but abounding towards the sea in remains of circular huts and other dry stone constructions, indicating a former ill-civilized but numerous population. Here, some distance up the mountain

Rathmalode.
Ord. Map,
Kerry.
45
*u. c.**

acclivity to the right, in the townland of Rathmalode, there formerly existed a Rath or earthen fort, and in it a cave, the lintel over the entrance to which, having on it a cross and an Ogham inscription, was transferred to the adjoining townland of Lougher, where it served the same purpose over the door of a farmer's dwelling until removed to the Royal Irish Academy, in Dublin, where it now is. We shall have

Rath cave.

occasion to notice many Rath-caves hereafter, and I may at once cite the compendious and interesting account of these constructions given by Colonel Lane Fox in his description of the Ogham-inscribed monuments found in the Rath-cave of Roovesmore, in the County of Cork:

" They (the forts or Raths) vary from 30 to 100 and 200 feet in diameter. The largest I know of in the south of Ireland, called Lisna-raha, has a diameter of 280 feet, with a ditch 12 feet deep, and 30 in width at the outside. . . . . . The interior space of the rath is almost invariably undermined by a set of chambers, ... the entrance to which is usually by an opening so small as barely to admit the body of a man creeping on the belly. These chambers vary in size, but average 9 feet in length by 3 to 4 in height, and the same in width. Similar narrow openings communicate onwards to the other chambers; and sometimes these underground galleries diverge into two or more strings of chambers, occupying the whole interior space within the circuit of the intrenchments. The main entrance is frequently in the ditch of the rath, and is not unusually the smallest. When the nature of the ground admits it, they are often excavated in the natural earth, and domed over without any artificial support; but others are

---

* Each sheet of the Ordnance Map of Ireland contains six square feet. To lighten the labour of searching so large a surface, the references are reduced to areas of a foot each; as

u. l.	*upper left.*	*u. c.*	*upper central.*	*u. r.*	*upper right.*
l. l.	*lower left.*	*l. c.*	*lower central.*	*l. r.*	*lower right.*

lined in the inside with undressed and uncemented stones, the sides KERRY (Corkaguiny). converging towards the top, which is usually flagged over with large and heavy slabs of stone, serving to roof the chamber, and, at the same time, by their weight, to prevent the sides from falling in; at other times, though rarely, they are formed by upright jambs of unhewn stone like the crypt at Roovesmore."

29. The inscription on the Lougher lintel is imperfect, but *Lougher* 45 *u. c.* enough remains to introduce us to one notable phrase in Ogham sepulchral legends.   It reads—

CURCIMAQIMUCOIF * *

and may obviously be divided

curci maqi mucoi f * *

that is, according to our present lights, (the stone) of Curc son of Mucoi F * * .   The meaning of *Mucoi* is still subject of speculation.   Haigh has taken it to mean ' daughter,' and would say that in this case before us ' Curc' should be regarded as ' son of the daughter of F * *,' according to the alleged Pictish system of tracing descent through the mother.   Brash has thought it a noun descriptive of the calling of the person designated, as swine-herd.   The late learned and ingenious Mr. Herbert, if he had been aware that a word suggestive of porcine meaning occurs in so old an inscriptional monument, would have recognised traces of that Early British Church organization in which, he thought, one of the grades was *porcus Christi.* Others have taken *mucoi* to mean " pure," " holy," " virgin."

30. Westward of Lougher, higher up in the recesses of the mountain, we come to a monument marked " Stone Cross " on *Ballynahunt* 45 *u. l.* the Ordnance Map, at a farmstead in the townland of Ballyna- hunt.   It stands attached to the gable of one of the farm build- ings, whither, I understand, it had been brought from a holy well higher up the mountain to the east.   The cross which gives it its name on the map is of considerable size, of the Latin form, incised on the broader end of the stone.   An Ogham inscription has occupied both arrises and the top of the narrower end. Were the stone set up, so as to exhibit the cross, the Ogham would be concealed in the earth.   This, however, is what we Ogham under ground. might be led to expect if we looked to our oldest written

Kerry
(Corkaguiny).
evidences for information regarding the form of such monuments, and the arrangement of Ogham legends on them.
There exists a remarkable romance—and a romance incidentally referring to such a matter is as good evidence as a
treatise—touching this subject, in our oldest Irish secular
manuscript, the Leabhar-na-h-Uidhre, compiled in the eleventh

Story of
Mongan.
century. The story turns on the identification of the burial-
place of Eochaid Argthec, a personage of third-century date.
In evidence of his having been buried at a particular place, one
of the actors in the piece is introduced as saying, "Take up the
stone that stands there. It bears his name. And the Ogham
that is written on the end of the stone that is in the earth is
this: *Eochaid Argthec innso*, Eochaid Argthec here." It may
be that the Ballynahunt inscription exemplifies this supposed
practice of hiding the sepulchral epigraph under ground; but
such is not found to have been the general practice. Other
examples, however, are not wanting of Ogham-inscribed flagstones laid flat on the surface, and this may very probably have
been one of that class. Whatever its age, the Ballynahunt

Monument
Christian.
stone, I make no doubt, is a Christian monument, not only
evidently by its cross—for I put aside the idea of Christian
crosses having been superadded to Pagan sepulchral monuments as resting on no evidence or reasonable presumption,—
but not improbably by the terms of the inscription itself.
The reading appears to be—

DUGENNGGELMAQıReDDoS.
U

which I would divide—

Dugennggel maqi reddos.

One digit only of what I suppose to be *l* remains at the top;
and, unless the character be *l*, the explanation of this strange
sequence of syllables which presented itself to my mind at the
time when I first examined the monument, must be discarded.

Disputation of
Proper Names.
I thought, then, the name might possibly be Dugreddos divided
by the interjected words *Ennggel maqi*, "apostle of the son,"
and not *Dugennyge* or *Dugennggnb*, "son of Reddos," as it has
by others been taken to be. Several examples of this kind of
word-intercalation, on the possibility of which I have here

speculated, are found in early Irish; as the verses improvised Kerry
by Columbkille on the death of Longarad of Killgarad (Fel. ^{(Corkaguiny).}
Æng, cxlii.)—

Is marb lon
do chill garad, mor in don——
Dead is Lon (of Cill) garad—great the evil !

where " do cill " is interposed between the constituent parts of
Longarad's name; and in the names of Cuchulain and Ferdiad,

Cu dan comainm *Culand*; and
Indar limsa *Fer* dil *diad*

in the Tain poems in the Book of Leinster. If other monuments shall appear to suggest something of the same kind of
dispartition of proper names, it will be well to bear the Ballynahunt legend in our recollection.

31. Near Annascaul, in the townland of Rathduff, lies the
Ballinvoher parish graveyard. A standing stone here bears the *Ballinvoher*
remains of Ogham characters now reported to be illegible. It ⁴⁵
l. l.
also bears a triple cross, incised. There seem to be no traces of
a church.

32. To the left of the highway, some distance from Annascaul, within the bounds of the parish of Ballinacourty, the
door lintel of a farmer's dwelling on the townland of Brackloon, *Brackloon*
if my memory serves me, bears another inscription, which Mr. ⁴⁵
l. l.
Brash (239) reads

Ercaficca maqi c. * *

The remainder is lost or possibly hidden in the masonry of the
wall. Not possessing a cast, and having mislaid my drawing,
it is with some misgiving I state my impression that the termination of the principal name is *ficcas*. It appears to be one of
a numerous class ending in *fec, fic,* and peculiar to the Counties
of Cork and Kerry.

33. At Ballintarmon, another townland in the same parish, *Ballintarmon*
is an Ogham-inscribed pillar, an account of which has been ⁴⁵
l. l.
published in Vallancey's " Collectanea," vol. vi., p. 224. A copy
of the text by Mr. Windele is published in Mr. Brash's work,
p. 200; but appears illegible. It bears a cross. I have not
seen it.

34. Entering on the parish of Minard, the general character of the country remains the same—a strip of two or three miles breadth between the mountains and the sea, rough, picturesque, and along the coast full of rude stone remains of old inhabitation. To the left of the highroad lies the townland of Gort-

negullanagh, from which one of the inscribed Ogham monuments now in the Academy's collection was removed many years ago. It formed a lintel over the doorway of one of the rude stone cloghans referred to. The stone is engraved on two angles, a boldly-cut cross between. One side reads

MAQQIDECEDDA.
Maqqi Decedda.

The other, imperfect at the end—

MAQQICATTUFic.
Maqqi Cattufic.

I do not find any other characters. Reading these as " the son of Decedd " on one side, and " the son of Catufic" on the other, the question naturally presents itself, How comes it that the persons intended to be commemorated are not themselves named, but only their fathers ? If there be no other answer than that such was a common style of epitaph in Oghamic times, as we shall see it was by frequent examples, it must be owned that our first entrance into the inquiry supplies us with a kind of sepulchral formula not easy to reconcile with the object of preserving individuals in monumental memory. We have no example of anything so vague in sepulchral *tituli* elsewhere, and may note the anomaly, especially in regard to the *maqqi decedda*, for future reference.

35. A highway to the coast, striking off from the main road at Gortnegullanagh, conducts to the adjoining townland of

Lugnagappul. Here, on the left hand of the road, at a place called Parknafulla, or the Field of Blood, is a low cairn once surrounded with standing stones, four of which remain, two being inscribed. I shall borrow Mr. Brash's description of the place and reading of the inscriptions, which I have not myself seen :—

" I . . . . . found a low cairn 30 ft. by 20 ft., of an irregular rectangular shape, composed of earth and stones, and from 2 ft. to 3 ft.

above the general level of the field. The two inscribed stones are on Kerry
the eastern side of the cairn. No 1 is a beautifully-formed pillar, oval (Corkaguiny).
in section and perfectly smooth, with a rounded top perfectly conical. Rounded pillar.
. . . . It is in length 4 ft. 2 in., its diameter being 1 ft. 5 in. and 1
ft 2 in. The inscription runs lengthwise on the centre of the stone,
without any stem line ; nevertheless, from the regularity and distinct-
ness of the characters, it is quite easy to recognise their values. It
commences at 1 ft. 9 in. from the bottom, and runs round the head—

Gossucttias.

. . . . . No 2 . . . . . stands on the same side of the cairn : it is a
flatter and more irregularly-shaped pillar than No. 1, being 4 ft. in
length, 1 ft. 3 in. in breadth, and 9 in. in thickness. The inscription
is on the rounded face near the centre running lengthwise upwards, and
occupying 1 ft. 10 in. in length, as follows—

Sticunas."
—(Og. Mon., 197–8.)

36. A sketch of Mr. Windele in his MS. which he entitles
" Iar Mumhain " (Lib. R.I.A.) resolves the *st* into *gam*, making

gamicunas,

apparently a more likely-looking combination.

37. The rounded pillar here described belongs to a type of
which we shall presently have many examples. Whether these
are artificially-shaped blocks or great rolled sea pebbles, I
cannot say. I do not know of their existence anywhere else
than in this immediate district, save in one instance where a
fragment of an inscribed pillar of the same kind was found on
the seacoast of Wexford, near Hook Point. The absence of a
stem-line is compensated by greater care in preserving the Line of con-
symmetry of the spacing, the vowels being shown by short vexity for
digits rather than notches, and the over-line and under-line stem line.
groups placed well apart from the middle convexity.

38. Proceeding from Lugnagappul towards the west, we
reach the townland and ruined church of Aglish, the cemetery *Aglish*
of which has furnished to the Lapidary Museum of the Royal 54
Irish Academy its much-canvassed *Apilogdo* inscription. Chris- *u. c.*
tian times are emphatically written on this stone by a Maltese
cross in a circle supported on a stem, at either side of which
may be discovered a filfot, a form of cross in Pagan as well as

KERRY
(Corkaguiny).

Christian use, but here made collateral and ancillary to the all-reconciling emblem. The Ogham characters at one side, if we may take them as complete, read

MAQIMAQ*A*
Maqi Maq*a*,

where we may again ask, What son? and who is *Maqa*, if that be the ending of this part of the legend ? At the other side, reading in like manner downward, we have

GD
APILOGGO
ST

where great embarrassment arises from the presence of an injured group of four stem-crossing digits, capable of many transliterations I at one time entertained the idea that, like the duplicate *Cellach* of the cypher, which reads both ways outward from a common centre, so, possibly, this legend is intended to be read both ways inward from the ends to the χ, making *Apostoli*; but this solution is far from satisfactory. Mr. Brash made, I think, a better guess in suggesting *Abilogus*, a well-known name both in Irish and Welsh annals. But the Bishop of Limerick has, perhaps, set us both right in seeking to identify the name as Aedloga, conceiving that it may be the record of Aedloga, son of Maeltuile, a petty king of the neighbouring territory, whose date would be sixth or seventh century. In making out the equivalence of these names, the Bishop treats the X character as having a third power, on the ground of *p*, *v*, and *dh*, passing into one another in numerous examples; and I am far from saying that he has not made a persuasive argument. In the same churchyard of Aglish still stands another Ogham-inscribed pillar. It does not appear to be now legible.

Aghacarrible
54
u. l.

39. From Aglish, in Minard, we cross the hill westward into the parish of Kinard, and reach the townland of Aghacarrible. This, in the other provinces of Ireland, would be called Aghacarble or Aghacarvil. The introduced vowel before *b* or *m* following *r* is still noticeable throughout Munster, and must be respected in such words as storm, form, farm, if we would not dislocate the prosody of the provincial poets. Even as late as the reign of Elizabeth, Carbery is spelt in official documents

Corribrie. Aghacarrible is regarded as a rath, rather than a killeen or burial-place, and it has a cave, similar to those described by Col. Lane Fox. What raises a doubt of its character as a rath is that just outside its circular ditch lies a great flagstone, apparently cast down from an erect position, covered with ring and cup decoration, arguing a monumental character. Taking it, however, as a rath, its cave may now claim our attention. It is but a few feet below the surface, about 5 ft. wide and 4½ ft. high. It consists of an outer and an inner chamber, walled at the sides with standing stones, and covered above with others laid across. Two of these wall stones bear Ogham legends—one, which I did not examine, is said to read

Maqi Bacos;

the other reads,

LADDIGNIMAQQIMUCCOIANA. * *
Laddigni maqqi muccoi ana. * *

where the remainder of the legend probably continues down the back arris, now inaccessible in the recesses of the wall. It is palpable that many of the supporting stones of such caves have been already inscribed with their Ogham legends before being built into their places; indeed in some of them the concealed characters can be felt with the hand. To read these legends fully, the roofing stones should be removed and the supporting wall stones exposed all round; but as yet, save at Dunloe, none have been more than very partially uncovered, and their legends remain in most cases to a great extent inaccessible. The patronymic name in this epigraph of *Laddignus* or *Laddignos* appears to begin with *Ana*, which, if so, would correspond with other seemingly classical names we shall meet with having the same prefix. The inference which commends itself most to the mind in contemplating such an interior is, that the materials already inscribed with their monumental epigraphs have been brought from some neighbouring cemetery; and this gives rise to a consideration of no little interest and curiosity. The cemeteries which are found adjoining such caves, and from which the materials of the caves have presumably been brought, are generally of that class of burial-places

KERRY
(Corkaguiny).
Killeens.
Not now used
for interment
of Christian
adults.

called *killeens* or *cealluraghs*. These are very numerous in the south and west of Ireland. They are not used for the interment of Christian adults. In most of them the burials are confined to unbaptised infants. Mr. Brash has given a highly curious and valuable account of them in his posthumous volume:—

" These cemeteries are to be distinguished from the ordinary burial-grounds of the country at present in use, and which are invariably connected with ancient churches or remains of a known Christian character. The keel is unconnected with Christian churches or associations of any kind, and, where still made use of, it is solely for the interment of unbaptized children and suicides. . . . . . They are usually circular areas of varying diameter, ... distinguished from the rath by having but one rampart without any ditch : the entrance is a cut through the fence. . . . . . In some instances the keel is enclosed by a circle of upright stones. . . . . . In some examples they are low circular or oval cairns, without any fence. . . . . . In many cases the mound and fence have been entirely erased, but . . . . . the site has been left to nature ; and, while the field around it has been a hundred times broken up and cultivated, nothing will induce the peasant to push a spade in or drive a plough through the keel. In some instances, in valuable land, the keel has been, from time to time, encroached on ; the cupidity of the farmer, getting the better of his superstitious fears, leads him to push his tillage, yard by yard, on the outward rim of the weird circle. The operation is quite evident at Kilcolaght in Kerry, and Kilgrovane in Waterford ; both bare circular, unenclosed and untilled spots in rich fields ; the Ogham-inscribed stones being huddled together in the centres."—(Og. Mon., 88.)

They are extraordinarily numerous in the Counties of Waterford, Cork, and Kerry. In the latter county, Mr. Brash enumerates under the denominations of Kill, Kyle, Killeen, Ccaluragh, and Children's Burial-grounds. one hundred and thirteen examples, besides one hundred and four old burial-grounds not now connected with any church. They are also numerous in the County of Antrim, in one parish of which, Culfeightrim,

" Dr. Reeves has identified nine of those keels, independent of the graveyards still in use "—(*Ib.*, 89.)

Mr. Brash concludes his very interesting notice of these

cemeteries, which he regards as wholly Pagan, by the state- KERRY
(Corkaguiny).
ment—

"In conversing with the peasantry of the south and west of Ireland,
I have never yet heard them use the word kıl to designate a church :
the word Teampuil is that invariably used by them, while the word keel
is always applied to the burial-grounds."—(*Ib.*, 92.)

How shall we account for the semi-sacred yet not quite holy
character of these cemeteries ?   The writers who assert a
Pagan origin for Ogham writing regard them as the burying-
places of the old Pagan population, and on this ground account
for the want of reverence for their gravestones shown by
those who plundered so many of them to obtain materials
for the construction of their rath-caves.   In support of this
view it is alleged that the Ogham inscriptions found in rath-
caves never bear the Christian emblem.   And this is generally
true.   We have seen, however, that the cross on the Gortnegullanagh stone did not protect it from being used as a lintel
over the doorway of the cloghan there; and, in fact, in this
cave of Aghacarrible one of the wall stones, although not *Aghacarrible*
Ogham-inscribed, bears two incised crosses, and has presumably,
as well as the others, been brought from some killeen or disused
cemetery in the neighbourhood.   The theory assumes a total
disuse of the Pagan cemeteries by the early Christians, save
for the interment of the unbaptised, which is not consistent
with the course of the social transition from Gentilism to the
Faith elsewhere.   Pagans and Christians repose in the adjoining
loculi of the Catacombs.   The repugnance indicated may have
sprung from another source, to which a wider survey of the
evidence may lead us further on.

40. Leaving Aghacarrible with its many hints to reflection,
we proceed to the townland of Kinard East, with its ruined *Kinard*
church and regular cemetery, containing two Ogham-inscribed   53
monuments.   One bears the name   *u. l.*

MARIANI,

with what appears an Oghamic alphabetic diagram annexed,
and an incised cross.   The other lies, as it seems designed to
have lain, on the surface of the ground.   It is inscribed along

the whole of one arris, over the head and down part of the arris opposite, and reads

ACURC₁T₁F₁NDDILORₐS
D   C
Acurc*iti* F*inddiloras*
d   c

which might be read *findiloras* or, allowing for the trans-position sometimes attending on the change from one arris to the other, *findidorac*. The name *Curcitt* will be sufficiently familiar to our eyes presently to induce the inquiry, What can be signified by the initial *a*? A sign of contraction (−⌢−) appears incised over it, and gives to this inscription the most modern aspect of any yet noticed. It possibly stands for an initial formula *anm*, of which we shall have many examples. So little did I regard it as part of the inscription when at Kinard in the commencement of these studies, that it has not been included in my cast, and its relevancy has only since become apparent to me. Note also the form of the inscription, importing that it is the memorial not of Curcitt son of Findi-loras or dorac, but in the possessive, of Curcitt's Findilora, or whatever the second name may be.

41. At Kinard we overlook the creek of Trabeg lying to the west, and, if it be low water, may see the *lac Sheevaun na geela*, as the Trabeg Ogham stone is popularly called, on the opposite beach. The *Bruscos* stone is a handsome pillar which formerly stood erect on the Garfinny or Dingle side of Trabeg, but now lies on the strand, where it is washed over at high water. The characters adjusted to one arris of the stone are easily legible, save towards the end of the inscription, where the carver has had to crowd his work somewhat to keep it from overrunning his space. Notwithstanding, some of the notches of his final group reach partly over the head of the stone. I made a careful cast of the whole in 1870, the photograph from which is preserved; but the light needed to bring the characters along the side into relief falling directly on the top, gives no shadow there, and, the cast having been lost or mislaid, I can only vouch my own recollection for the existence of the terminal *i* of the legend. It reads

BRUSCOSMAQICALIₐCI
&c.
Bruscos Maqi Cal*iaci*,

or *Caluoci,* according as the notches following the *l* are regarded KFRRY
as six or five in number. If five, the apparent hiatus in the (Corkaguiny).
group divides it into *u* and *o.* But the seeming hiatus to my
eye betrays the remains of an abraded sixth notch, and the
reading results, as in Divitiacus, *Caliaci,* which seems most
probably a statelier presentation of the ordinary name *Cellach.*

42. This creek of Trabeg is the first indentation in the
long coast-line from Slieve Mish. It is followed by the land-
locked sheet of Dingle harbour, two miles west ; and this
again, at a less interval, by the equally capacious and sheltered
harbour of Ventry. About the centre of the peninsula, between
Trabeg and the harbour of Dingle, on a byroad to the left,
stands the *Killeen* of Ballintaggart or Priesttown. The church *Ballintaggart*
and regular cemetery are at a little distance. It is a rough 53
u. c.
circle about 60 ft. in diameter, surrounded by a ditched fence.
The access is by a gap on the north. On entering, one perceives
no fewer than eight of those rounded pebble-like blocks of which
some account has been given at Lugnagappul, laid on the surface
round the margin of the enclosure. They do not appear ever
to have stood upright, but the tops and bottoms, alike rounded
and still in some degree polished, are distinguishable by the
direction of their legends, which occupy the sides and tops
only. These oblate flattened stone spheroids are most difficult
to cast in paper. The mould must be made in several parts;
otherwise it will not come off without tearing, and the junctures
of these pieces where the loss or duplication of a digit may
work transformations so extensive, is a business of excessive
nicety. Add to this the incidents of windy or rainy weather
and the awkwardness of inexperienced hands, and it will not be
matter of surprise that the casts of these pulvinarian cope-
stones, taken by myself and the late Mr. Burchett, exhibit many
imperfections. The sharpness of the casts, indeed, has in
many cases been blurred by the necessity of carrying them in a
wet state to where they could be dried at a fire. Were the
work to do again, I would advise the employment of plaster of
Paris, from which paper casts might be taken at leisure under
cover; for the plaster cast cannot be turned to the light or
examined with at all as profitable a scrutiny as the light and
easily-handled piece of *papier maché.* Still, with their help, I

Kerry
(Corkaguiny).

Ballintaggart
(A)

think I can answer for the transliteration of these eight legends.

43. Beginning with the first stone to the left, one is struck with the peculiar tridental form of the ends of the arms and stem of the cross, incised on its smooth upper convexity. The digits of the accompanying inscription are broad and symmetrical. On the north or right side, beginning from below, is the same name lately noticed at Kinard,

CURCITTI.

On the opposite side, beginning also from below and rounding the top, the legend reads

TRIAMAQAMAILAGNI
Tria Maqa Mailagni.

Here we have an example of *Maqa* uncomplicated by any doubt as to the finality of the *a*. Nothing is disputed save whether *Mailagni* should not be read *Meolagni*. The undivided six notches might be read either way, or they might be read *uu*, or *uoa*, or in various other combinations if the form of the name so required. But the question for more serious consideration is whether the *maqa* here is a feminine, in agreement with *Tria*, and the same with the seeming *Maqa* of the Aglish stone? Then, *Tria*, is it a personal name or a numeral, a singular or a plural? I wish I could answer, or even hold out the hope that materials for an answer may be expected in our further course of investigation. But, copious as the general material is, it, as yet, supplies no further example of similar endings in *a*, and I abstain from conjecture.

Ballintaggart
(B)

44. The second of this strange group of monuments supplies, if not a new word, a new phonetic element in nomenclature, which will often recur. The legend, beginning at the bottom lefthand side of the stone, runs continuously over the top and down the other side, having a plain cross on the space between. Its reading is complicated by the presence of the X character, to which, so far, we have seen, two values are generally allowed to be assignable—the diphthong in *e*, as *ea*, *eo*, &c, and *p* It is plain, from the concurrence of vowels flanking the X, that it cannot be the diphthong here; and, by giving to

it its *p* value, this is the transliteration which appears to KERRY
result— (Corkaguiny).

NETTALMINACCAPUIMAQQiMuCOIDOros
EA
&c.

Nettal minacca *p*ui maqqi mucoi Do(*ros*).

We easily segregate the now familiar *maqqi mucoi*; but the *netta*
or *nettal* and the *pui* are new. Whether the *netta* is to be taken " *nettal* "
as parcel of a proper name, or as an independent vocable, or to
be read as *ettal* preceded possibly by the article *an*, are questions
as hard to solve as any we are likely to encounter. I had
first no doubt that it formed part of a proper name, *Nettalami*,
but the cast refuses to admit an *a* after the *l*, and compels us to
read *ettal minacca*, which certainly calls up the idea of Italian
monachism. The *poi* or *pui* stands independently in the place " *pui* "
where we might expect the *copula* in the sentence, and presents
the welcome feature of something predicative. It is, in fact,
the verb substantive in the past tense. We shall often meet it
in the form *poi*, corresponding to the Irish *boi*, that is *fuit*,
" was " or " who was." I make no doubt that the Bishop of
Limerick is quite well grounded in this discovery, and that
whether it be an Italian religious who is here commemorated
or some one called *Netlam (Nitida Manus)*, the legend asserts
he or she " was " *Maqqi Mucoi Do(ros)*, whatever that may
mean.

45. The third of the group, giving its *p* force to the second *Ballintaggart*
character, reads (C)

APEFRITTI,

which seems to designate a son of *Efritt. Efritt, Efratt*, is a name
known in Patrician documents. The *ap* therefore may be an
early form of the Welsh *map*, the equivalent of the Irish *maqi*.
But the question presents itself, Whence came the employment of *p*,—a letter not in the original Ogham alphabet,—here
as well as on the preceding and on the Aglish monument? There
were two lines of British connection with Munster—one before
the introduction of Patrician Christianity; the other, through
the Welsh ecclesiastics who came in some Patrick's train. The
first connection rests on both British and Irish authority dating Use of the
from the time of Nennius; the second appears by a curious letter *p*.

D

KERRY
(Corkaguiny).

passage in the Glossary of Cormac, to the effect that the Welsh-men who came with Patrick could not pronounce the Irish word *Cruimthir* (corrupted from *Presbyter*, a Priest), but called it *Premter*. According as the *p's* of these inscriptions shall be referred to the one or the other of these origins will be the length of the retrospect which materials of the kind now before us may justify us in taking.

Ballintaggart
(D)

46. The fourth member of the group offers the first example, so far. of vowels being indicated throughout the greater part of the text by stem-crossing digits equally long as those employed for consonants. This adds materially to the risk of error in transliteration ; but, the legend being confined to vowels and underline consonants, the difficulty is less felt.

INISSIMONAS.

If the name be *Ssimon*, we might recognise, in the initial *ini*, a reflection of the *inso* of Eochaid.

Ballintaggart
(E)

47. This is one of the most clearly inscribed and easily transliterated of the group.   It reads

MAQQIIARIPOIMAQQIMUCCOıDoFFINIAS
EA
&c.

Maqqi Iari poi maqqi muccoi Doffinias.

The name Iar, father of the father of four virgins, stated to be venerated " at Cell Ingen Iaráin and in Corkaguiny," occurs in the Feliré of Ængus (Fel. Æng., 26 Oct , Trans. R I.A. Ir. Ser., vol. i , clix.)   Iar's father is named and described in the inscription; but neither in it nor in the Feliré is any further designation given to Iar's son. *Maqi Iari* may therefore be supposed to have been a person of sufficient distinction to have been remembered as son—perhaps only son—of his father. Or it may be that such formulas were in use when the son was called after the father, or by a diminution of the father's name, as in " Cell Ingen Iaráin."

Ballintaggart
(F)

48. Offers nothing questionable.   It is the simple record—

DOFETIMAQQICATTINI
Dofeti maqqi Cattini.

which doubtless preserves the name of Dofet, son of Cattin.

49. The same formula is preserved in the seventh of the KERRY (Corkaguiny). group.

SUFALLOSMAQQIDUCOFAROS *Ballintaggart*
Sufallos maqqi Ducofaros. (G)

The Greekish aspect which struck us in other names again appears in *Ducofaros*. There is reason for thinking these *os* terminations indeclinable. They are found to be so in the Greek proper names adopted into Eastern liturgies. Both Egyptians and Greeks are known to have resorted to Ireland in early monastic times, and it may well be, as the Bishop of Limerick has supposed, that these *os* loan-terminations are traces of their presence, and are no more declinable here than in the Coptic.

50. We have now made the round of the *Killeen*, and have reached the stone which lay at the right-hand on entering. On one side it repeats the *maqqi decedda* of Gortnegullanagh in *Ballintaggart* the form (H)

MAQIDECCEDA
Maqi Decceda.

The word *Decced* is not anywhere found in the nominative in these monuments, which may excite some doubt whether it is a proper name. The inscription on the opposite side, beginning from below and rounding over the head of the stone, presents what seems to be a pair of names conceived in the possessive formula A's B, as on Curcitt's stone at Kinard. The traces on the top of the stone are extremely faint, but along the side are strongly cut and almost all certain—

OLUSSESICONAS,
or, if taken in the reverse sequence,

CAQOSICECCUDO(ros?)
Caqosi ceccudo(ros),

and must be regarded as preserving names very singular in their apparent meanings.

51. A ninth Ogham-inscribed monument lies outside the *Ballintaggart* Killeen to the south. It is of the arrised class, very rugged, (I) and in some places hard to transliterate, but appears to read—

COLUMMAQQIFIC(ias)
B
Colum maqqi Fic(*ias*).

Here, unless we suppose the *m* to play a double part, the reading would be *Columbaqqific* (&c.), but the upper half of the *b* digit may well be supposed to have been lost.

52. Returning to the main road which conducts from Lispole Bridge at the head of the Creek of Trabeg to the town of Dingle, about two miles out of the town, close to the highroad on the left, in the townland of Ballynesteenig, is seen another, and the last, as it is also the largest, of the lenticular class of monument which we have still to notice. It remains nearly in the same place where it lay when seen by Mr. Pelham early in this century. It was then whole, a rounded pillar-like block with semi-spheroidal ends of about $7\frac{1}{2}$ ft. in length. It has since been broken in two by kindling a fire against it, but the fracture has not injured the inscription, which is boldly incised along the medial convexity—

MOINENAMAQIOLACON
Moinena maqi olacon.

It was early pointed out by the Bishop of Limerick that Moinena is a well-known name borne by several ecclesiastics, and Olacon, the genitive of Olchu, an equally well-known proper name. He went further, and showed that an Olchu was grandfather of St Brendan, and that a Moinena who died in the year 571, was the bishop attached to St. Brendan's monastery at Clonfert. That he should have been interred in Brendan's ancestral district seems not improbable, and certainly no one can reasonably, in presence of such facts, question the appropriateness of the cross which accompanies the inscription.

53. Just on the outskirts of Dingle a laneway to the left leads through the townland of Emlagh West, where stands the fragment of a pillar bearing the legend—

TALAGNIMAQ
C
Talagni maq(i).

Talagni, like the *Laddigni* of Aghacarrible and *Mailagni* of Ballintaggart, seems to be the genitive of a proper name. We shall find many examples of similar forms. They appear to imply Oghamic nominatives in *os*. It seems agreed on that the representatives of those in *agni* at the present day would be forms in *án*, such as Tallán, Bonán, &c.

54. The country around Dingle offers a marked contrast to the rugged tract through which it has been approached. Across the lake-like harbour is seen the lofty residence of Lord Ventry at Burnham. Lord Ventry has assembled here a collection of Ogham-inscribed monuments, which I purpose to describe in connection with their places of origin ; proceeding at once to the rich Oghamic tract which lies to the north and west.

KERRY (Corkaguiny).

Burnham House

55. Two miles north-west from Dingle on the Kilmalkedar road, to the left, is the Killeen and ruined church of Kilfountain, with its monumental pillar. Mr. Brash states that what remains of the church is in dry-stone masonry. There are many Fintans, generally spelled Fionntain in the Irish Calendars ; but the name as it appears on this monument in Roman characters is Finten. It is inscribed under a characteristic Celtic cross, accompanied by singular and not inelegant ornamentation ; and there are, adjoining it, along the arris of the stone, three Ogham characters, INS, wanting only *o*, which may have been there to make the *inso* we have been in search of. It is one of the rare instances in which a Killeen is found in connection with existing ruins of a church, and with an evidently Christian monument erected in it. Being Christian and presumably consecrated, why, it may be asked, is the cemetery now regarded as unfit for adult Christian burial ? and why and when did it come to be so regarded ? Whether any answer can be given to these questions must depend on a fuller survey of the remaining evidences; but enough has been seen already to give these Killeens a wider interest than they may at first have appeared to possess.

Kilfountain 43 l. l.

56. From Kilfountain, a by-road leading westward conducts to the townland of Maumanorigh, where will be found another children's burial-place, and in it the foundations of a ruined church and a stone monument bearing an Ogham legend of a more complex, and, so far, a novel character. That it is a Christian monument is attested by two Maltese crosses, one of them supported on a stem, as on the Aglish example. The inscription is carried round the face of the stone, which is a boulder apparently *in situ,* on an artificially cut stem-line, and

Maumanorigh 42 l. r.

KERRY
(Corkaguiny).

at first sight appears to present the following singular succession of syllables—

ANMCOLOLOMBNALILTER
L
anm Cololomb nalilter.

Maumanorigh

The introductory *anm* occurs on so many other examples that it is easily separable from what seems the principal name beginning with *col*. I at one time thought the *anm* and *col* were to be read both ways, outward from c, as in the puzzle-cypher of *cellach*, yielding the name Colman, to which I was encouraged by the fact of the adjoining townland, which might have included Maumanorigh as a sub-denomination, being called Kilcolman, and of there being no church or burial ground there; and taking the name to be Colman, there seemed good reason for recognising in the terminal groups, slightly altered, the word *ailitir*, "pilgrim." I had, however, to abandon this ancillary use of *anm*, on finding that combination of letters to be, as it is, a common formula prefixed to many other Ogham inscriptions, and the great difficulty of the intermediate *cololol* still remained. A closer scrutiny, however, of the text seemed to restore *Colman* in another form; for what at first sight seemed the terminal *l* before *nalilter*, having part of its first digit above the stem, might resolve itself into *mb*, making *Cololomb*, and the interjected syllable *ol* only remained to be dealt with. In this stage of the investigation my friend, Dr. Whitley Stokes, threw upon it the light which is only to be had from very rare learning and research in manuscript originals. He found in the Library of Trinity College, Dublin (H 2, 15), in the handwriting of Dudley MacFirbis, a tract called

Duil Laithne.

Duil Laithne, containing a class of words fabricated by a process called *formolad*, from ordinary Irish words, either by inserting certain meaningless syllables, or by substituting certain letters for others. The inserted syllables, of which the *Duil Laithne* affords examples, are *osc, anc, inc, unc, nro, ucull, ros, es* or *os, air, aur, ur,* and *oll,* as *collumac,* "power," formed on the Irish *cumac; colluicen,* "kitchen," formed on the Irish *cuicenn;* just as here, by the same process, the sculptor of the Maumanorigh Ogham appears to have engraved *Cololomb* for the Irish Colomb. The *l* in the *nalilter* I would suppose to be a super-

fetation of the same kind, and conclude that "Columb the KERRY
pilgrim" is the person in whose epitaph these pains have been (Corkaguiny).
taken to disguise his name and manifest his Christian
labours. We will not be surprised, after this, to learn that
the Uraicapt, or what is called the Primer of the Bards,
enumerates no fewer than eight *bearla* or forms of speech, one *Maumanorigh*
of which, the *bearla tobaid*, seems to be formed by additions
of some and droppings of other letters. All this sounds very
fanciful and unlikely to have existed in practice among a
people having the ordinary occasions for the use of language.
But in an isolated community with various castes and orders
of society such a thing may be conceived of; and we may
not altogether discredit the story of King Conor MacNessa,
who, having heard his judges debate a question in language
unintelligible to him and the bystanders, enacted that in the
administration of justice for the future the language used
should be the vernacular of the day.

57. Columb appears to have been a favourite name among
the religious of Corkaguiny. Petrie has given a drawing of the
stone of another Columb not far from Maumanorigh, in his
essay. I cite it here for the sake of its monogram of Maria,
which it exhibits in conjunction with what seems to be the
almost obliterated name of Colum, son of Mal——, in Roman
characters.

58. Two miles distant, to the north-west, near the Dunurlin *Cahirnagat*
road, in the townland of Ballywiheen, we come on a way-side 42
pile of stones called Cahir-na-gat or Cats' Castle, surmounted *l. c.*
by a pillar found in an adjoining Killeen. Its legend is almost
unique in its completeness and the certainty of all its digits—

TOGITTACCMAQISAGARETTOS
Togittacc maqi Sagarettos.

If *maqi* be a genitive, as we have hitherto accepted it, then
it cannot be in agreement with the nominative Togittacc, and
the reading must be Togittaccus Sacerdos Filii, a highly
Christian and doctrinal meaning, quite in accordance with
what has been seen respecting the names in *os* already
observed on. But if any doubt whether *maqi* be not necessarily genitive have arisen, this, for its solution, will await

KERRY
(Corkaguiny). us and the Atlantic.

our arrival at the next monument but two remaining between us and the Atlantic.

Temple Mana-
han
42
l. c.
59. At a short distance, north, in the same townland are the *Cealluragh*, cell, and monumental pillar of Temple Manahan. This also is a children's burial-place, and it contains one of those dry-stone cells or oratories with which Petrie has made us familiar in his essay on Irish ecclesiastical architecture. A rude causeway leads to the door of this little structure. To the right of the causeway stands Saint Manchan's pillar, inscribed with two crosses and its Ogham legend. A fracture at the top has carried away some digits and notches, but you will readily supply the remainder of the lost formula. What remains reads—

QENELOCIMAQIMAQIAINIAMUCOI
T
Qeneloci maqi maqi ainia mu*coi*.

What may have followed *Mucoi* must remain unknown, but it looks as if it were the end of the legend. If this be Manchan's epitaph, he is presented to us by his secular name, which might be surmised to have been Cennloc, Cennlogha, or something similar. He is made son of the son of Ainia, a name not known to me elsewhere. The crosses may sufficiently testify to his having been a Christian. Why, then, the question will recur, should his cemetery now, like his neighbour Fintan's, be disparaged by the faithful and reserved for the unbaptised?

Tyvoria
42
l. l.
60. The intermediate monument referred to stands near the high road at Tyvoria, in the townland of Teeravona. It does not bear an Ogham inscription of the ordinary kind; but is noticed on account of its monogram corresponding to that on the Colomb stone, accompanied with a device somewhat resembling the one at Kinard, and probably an Oghamic biliteral echo of *Maria*.

Clogher Head
or Dunmore
42
l. l.
61. At Tyvoria we are near the sea-shore, and, taking the coast road southward, reach Dunmore Head. On the ridge of the promontory, in a conspicuous position over the Atlantic, stands a pillar-stone bearing the Ogham legend, on one arris—

Q
ERCMAQIERCIAS
Erc maqi Ercias.

and on the other, after intermediate characters not now legible, the name, already noticed elsewhere, KERRY (Corkaguiny).

DOFINIAS.
A

Up almost to this point we have regarded *maqi* as a genitive. The suffixed *i* has been considered inflectional and equivalent to the infixed *i* of *maic*, the more modern genitive of *mac*. Here it appears indisputably to be in agreement with the nominative *Erc*, and excites renewed doubts as to these Oghamic forms being governed by ordinary grammatical laws. The *ias* genitive for nouns ending in *c* and *n* is again exemplified in this inscription, which, rugged and weather-worn as it is, must be considered one of the most valuable for philological use, or warning, as the case may be, hitherto noticed.

" Maqi " seemingly in the nominative.

CHAPTER III.

KERRY.
Ballyneanig
42
n c.

62. TURNING back from Dunmore Head, and proceeding in the direction of Smerwick Bay and the heights of Brandon, we pass the lands of Ballyneanig, which have supplied one of the Ogham examples at the Academy. It is imperfect, but, I think, accepting in part Mr. Brash's correction of a former reading of my own, may be rendered—

.165

LUGIQRITTIMA(QI).
Qritti.

Lucrit would not strike the eye as an abnormal form of an Irish name ; and it may be, here, it is presented in state-dress.

63. We are here in sight of the harbour of Smerwick lying between us and the acclivities of Mount Brandon. Its shores are barren and solitary. A broad sandy beach curves round its inland margin. On a low promontory about the middle of this beach, in the townland of Ballinrannig, formerly stood seven Ogham-inscribed monumental pillars. Whether the site was a *cealluragh* or a cemetery attached to a church cannot now be determined, the blowing sands have so overspread it. Mr. Windele visited the place in 1838, and made a highly characteristic sketch of it as it then appeared. Of the seven pillars, one only remains *in situ*, now prostrate and concealed

Ballinrannig
42
n. c.

in the sand. I have not seen it. Transcripts by various KERRY.
hands make it—

Cunas maqqi Corli maqqi—

and

Cona maqqi Corbbi maqqi—

I adduce it here partly on account of the name *Cunas* or *Cona*, which may find an echo further on, but chiefly as introductory to a peculiar class of proper names, of which we shall have frequent examples. Having regard to these, I would observe that *Corb* appears more likely to be an Ogham proper name than Corl, as having a meaning "bad," "wicked," the relevancy of which will now receive some illustration. The pillar which, in 1838, occupied the summit of the knoll, is now, I believe, at Burnham, having been removed from Lough, *Burnham* near Ballintaggart, where I saw it in 1870. It bears, (A) distinctly cut, the name

BROINIUNAS,
Broiniunas,

where the *as* genitive instead of the *ias* of other examples may invite the attention of the grammarian. *Broinion*, as a proper name, seems to import, like Corb, personal depreciation. We are here, I think, on the track of an explanation of other apparently humiliatory designations, the singularity of which made us pause for a moment over one of the Ballintaggart group. One of the most curious contributions to inscriptional criticism of our day is a paper by M. Edmond Le Blant in the *Revue Archæologique* (N.S. x. 5), entitled "*Sur quelques noms bizarres adoptés par les premiers Chrétiens*," in which he treats of certain names of self-depreciation and reproach assumed by Christian devotees from the fourth to the eighth century. Amongst others he enumerates—

Contumeliosus	Fœdulus
Injuriosus	Maliciosus
Importunus	Molesta
Malus	Pecus
Exitiosus	Fimus
Calumniosus	Stercus
Insapientia	Stercorius

Hence it may appear that the Irish lexicographer MacCurtin, when he wrote the following paragraph of his treatise on Oghamic writing annexed to his Dictionary, was not altogether without foundation for his statement, however puerile in the way he puts it, that matters to the disparagement of the deceased were often contained in their Ogham epitaphs. " It was penal," he says, " for any but those that were sworn Antiquaries to study or read the same. For in these characters those sworn Antiquaries wrote all the evil actions and other vicious practices of their monarchs and other great personages, both male and female, that it might not be known to any but themselves, being sworn Antiquaries, as aforesaid." Hence, also, a probable cause may be surmised for the frequent obliteration of parts of Ogham legends, leaving the *Maqi's* and *Mucoi's* untouched.

Burnham
(B)

` **64.** Three other of the original pillars are also at Burnham. On one of those I thought I traced the remains of the name *Gillamurra* or *Gillamurras* in continuation of *Maqi Tenac*— on the opposite angle

MAQQITENAC
GıLLAMURRas.

The Christian form of *Gillamurras* excited much controversy. It still seems to me the likeliest reconstruction of the text, which notably illustrates what has already been said of the inherent ambiguities of this kind of writing ; for it depends altogether on whether the second digit of what otherwise would be an *i* of five notches has not extended on both sides of the arris, turning *i* into *amu*. The digit in question is shorter than that which, taken as *m*, helped us over the puzzle of *Colomb* at Maumanorigh ; and both are under the usual length of that letter, although distinctly crossing the arris.

Burnham
(C)

65. Another follows the example of the Gortnegullanagh example, giving apparently only the patronymics—

MAQQICUNITTI.
MAQQI QITTI.

The third is imperfect at foot, but preserves the form—

$_{G}^{B}$RAFICASMAQIMUCOI.

(g)raficas maqi mucoi,

where we see again the genitive in *as* instead of *ias* of other KERRY.
examples, and may note the terminal *mucoi* for future ·refer- gen. in *as*
ence. *mucoi* terminal

66. Of the Chute Hall group I cannot speak from personal
knowledge. I have seen several readings of one made by
gentlemen of skill and experience, but greatly discrepant, and
do not reproduce it. Of the other, all the copies I have seen
agree—

Ccicamini maqqi cattini.

Cucuimne is the name of an Irish person recorded in the *Liber
Hymnorum*, and, if I might be so bold, I would submit that
Cicamin gives a more probable foundation for the name of
the Broch, *Dun-Clicamin*, than the local circumstance which
has been suggested to account for it.

67. Leaving the cairn of *Cill-Vickallane,* or "the Grave-
yard of the Sons," as this solitary spot is still called, amid
its waste of sand and water, we may now direct our steps
to Kilmalkedar, from the road to which place we began so
long a divergence when turning westward at Kilfountain. *Kilmalkedar*
Here we find a comparatively large Christian church of that 42
Hiberno-Romanesque style which Petrie has endeavoured *u. l.*
to show was earlier developed in Irish than in British
examples. Surrounding it is a regular church cemetery
crowded with the gravestones of perhaps thirty generations,
under no popular interdict, and where the unbaptised and
suicide would not be admitted. Among the other standing-
stones marking the graves of the Faithful, is one pillar Ogham-
inscribed, and which, when I first examined it, appeared to
confirm my impression of the tenor of the Ballinahunt legend.
It seemed to read "angel" before the principal name, but too
obscurely to justify me in a published transliteration. On
the cast it is seen that *an* and what may be two *m's* or a
widely-spaced *g*, with room for a considerable number of
abraded vowel points, precede the letter *l* in the introductory
part of the legend. This may be the frequent initial formula
anm followed by *Mael* or *Maoil inbiric*, with an interjected X
after *Maoil*; or it may be "angeil" followed by X. I have
to thank Mr. Brash, for suggesting the former reading, which
now seems to me the preferable one. But what shall we

make of the X?   In none of the values hitherto given it, will it fall in with the context, and must, I imagine, be regarded as a non-vocable symbol thrown in out of a superfluous piety among the constituents of the name, as on Norse bracteates and Anglo-Saxon coins of the later middle ages.   The whole legend, then, would now appear to run, including what may be considered doubtful in brackets—

Right arris—   AN^{M Maoi}_{G   e}LINBIRɪc.

Left   „   MACIBROCANɪaS.
          Anmmaoilinbir[ic] maci brocani[as].

The *Brocani* or *Brocanias*, as I think it was engraved, might be expected in the form *Brocagni*, and possibly we have here a transition from an older to a more modern inflexional form, a conjecture countenanced by the substitution of *c* for *q* in *maci*.

Gallerus
42
u. l.

68.   Before leaving this Kilmalkedar district we may observe the remarkable *cell* or primitive dry-stone church at *Gallerus.* It is a small edifice with sloping sides rounding into a Gothic arched roof surmounted by a crest or barge-course of masonry ; and exactly corresponds in outline with one of the Roman miniature cellæ preserved at Nancy, which I am about to refer to.   We must have been struck with the fact that, save at Kilmalkedar and Kinard, all the cemeteries, *kills, killeens,* and *cealluraghs* so far noticed are either without any trace of churches or, in exceptional cases, as at Kɪlfountain and St. Manchan's, are associated with edifices little removed from the rude *cloghans* of the country.   In regard to these churchless burying places, it might be thought that wooden churches may have stood in or near them formerly, and may have been consumed by Time.   But this is an exceptionally stone building district.   From Ventry west the seacoast is covered with the drystone ruins of what is called "the city of Fahan," and the whole tract thence to Kilmalkedar is full of stone monuments.   The existence, however, of cemeteries without churches need excite no surprise. If these were, as seems most probable, Pagan places of burial originally, there would be no ground for expecting annexed buildings of either wood or of stone.   What is surprising in

connection with them is how they came to be called *kill* and KERRY.
killeen, equivalent to "church," and "little church," or "chapel."
In the Irish of the middle ages the *kill* of topography is *cell*, the
equivalent of—I do not at all say derived from—the Latin
cella. *Cella* is primarily a cellar or place of deposit; in its
secondary sense the cell or shrine of a temple, the separate
dwelling of a monk, &c. It is not used in the meaning of a *Kill* and
sepulchre in any literary record, so far as I know, but in early *Killeen*
Christian symbolic sculpture it is so represented. Lazarus in sepulchral.
the catacombs and on the sarcophagi always issues from the
portico of a little cell or temple-like structure, sometimes
ridge-roofed, sometime domed like a Byzantine basilica.
What indicates the connection this seems to have with the *kills*
and *killeens* of Corcaguiny comes not inappropriately from the
Leges Barbarorum. In the Salique Law of Graves—"If
anyone throw down or plunder the *porticulus* set up over a
dead person;" "If anyone shall pillage the house made in the
form of a *basilica* over a dead person;" "If anyone burn a
basilica over a dead person," let him pay a fine of so much.
Down to later than mediæval times the representative of
these Frankish *porticuli* and *basilicæ* in Provence were called
chapels, and appear to have been of wood. In Pagan times
they had been of stone. There is an assemblage of such
objects in stone in the Burgundian Museum at Nancy. They
are miniature *Ædiculæ* of 2 or 3 ft. in height, bearing Roman
inscriptions with D. M. prefixed, and exhibit all the characteristic forms of the stone cells and early stone churches, as well
as of the sepulchral stone vaults, of these southern and
western Irish places of burial. The name of the cell-like
structure over the sepulchre passing to the burial-place,
might account for these Irish *kills* having been so called,
although without associated churches. There is some
authority for the suggestion. *Feretrum*, a bier, in the Origines
of Isidore, is "the *place* to which the dead are borne," and
it is not improbable that the Irish "*feart*," in its sense of a
"grave," may be of the same origin. I read some curiously
corroborative matter in Colonel Forbes Leslie's "Ancient
Races of Scotland." He points out that several stone circles
and remains of burying places, apart from any place of

worship, continue to be known by the names "church," "kirk," and "chapel"; and I may add that the MacMahon burial vault, at Inniskeen, in Monaghan, bears an inscription purporting that "this chapel" was erected by, &c. We may consequently conclude that we have up to the present been mainly among the traces of a Christian church, which, as regards places of worship, was churchless, or, at least to some extent, a church of catacomb organisation. It is now time to resume the survey which next leads eastward over Brandon mountain.

69. On the western shoulder of Mount Brandon, which rises precipitously from the sea, there is a comparatively level *plateau* forming a terrace between the verge of the cliff and the central summit of the mountain further south. Here in the townland of Arraglen, at a height of upwards of 2,000 ft., stands the "cruimthir" pillar. Excepting the foundation of a modern signal tower, there is no trace of habitation within miles, save the ruined hermitage of St. Brendan, 1,000 ft. higher on the ridge behind. Two crosses, one on the front, the other, a Maltese cross in a circle, on the back of the pillar, sufficiently attest its Christian character. Up the seaward arris of the western front runs an Ogham legend, about which, save its last latter, there is no difference of judgment.

QRIMITIRROS,

whether the last letter be *s* or *n* is doubtful. If *n*, it will read, in continuation, as part of the proper name *Ronan Maq Comogann* on the arris opposite. If *s*, which I cannot help taking it to be, the legend would run—

QRIMITIRROS AN MAQ COMOGANN,

certainly not so satisfactory as Haigh's reading, which yields the name Ronan as that of the *crumthir*.

70. Proceeding along the seaward face of the mountain, we reach a stream on its eastern declivity, crossed by Tier Bridge, and descending towards the coast village of Cloghane, in the townland of Clonsharagh, come on three great *gallauns* or standing stones. They stand in line, and measure 7 ft., 10 ft., and 12 ft. above ground respectively. Their aspect is certainly not such as our present information would lead us to expect in Christian monuments. A fourth, now prostrate, has KERRY. formerly stood to the left. The rude, massive character of the stones, and the sternness and solitude of the situation, make a profound impression on the mind. Ogham digits exist on the side and top arris of the great block in the centre of the standing group. They are scattered, and not legible; but if Christianity be plainly written in Ogham on the Arraglen pillar, the same certainly cannot be said of this Ogham-marked *Gallaun* of Clonsharagh.

71. We now leave Brandon mountain, which at this side presents a vast grassy concavity, surmounted by a wall of rock under Brendan's hermitage, and proceed eastward to Castlegregory, in Killaney parish. Here, in the townland of Martramane, built into the chimney-breast of a farmer's *Martramane* cottage, formerly existed an inscribed stone, said to have been $\frac{36}{u.\ l.}$ brought from one of the Magheree Islands in the offing, now in the collection of the Royal Irish Academy. Its legend, imperfect at the end, will recall the *Qeniloci* of St. Manchan's.

QENILOCGNIMAQID——.
Qenilocgni maqi d——.

72. There remains but one other Ogham inscription, so far as my knowledge goes, in Corkaguiny. We reach it about five miles further eastward, in the townland of Camp, near *Camp* where the Castlegregory road is met by the line from Anas- $\frac{37}{l.\ r.}$ caul. We are here again under the western declivity of Slieve Mish. If we ascended the valley, which at this side skirts the foot of the mountain, we would find the ruined barbaric fortress of Cahir Conree at the summit. This means the fort of Curoi (making *conree* in the genitive) son of Dari, a name famous in Irish romance, the contemporary and rival of Cuchullin, by whom he was slain in his mountain stronghold, through the treachery of the faithless Blanaid. She milked the fatal white cows with the red ears, which Cuchullin and Conall Carnach had plundered from Eochy Eachbeol, King of Scotland, into the stream running down hither, which was the signal for the attack. Here, to the east of the Anascaul-road, on the surface of the ground, is seen a great flattish block, like the covering stone of a cromlech round which the soil had accumulated. It bears a

E

cross and an inscription in Roman characters, as well as an Ogham legend on the edge remote from the road. Read from left to right in the usual manner, it yields the transliteration—

SOQUQCEAFFMONISOQURI,

and remained unexplained until the present Bishop of Limerick (then Rev. Dr. Charles Graves) perceived that the characters are inverted, and that the reading really is—

Conuneatt maqi Conuri,

or, it may be,

Conun eattmaqi Conuri.

The cross and the Roman letters forbid our thinking of the son of Dari, but it is difficult to dissociate the name from that of Curoi, Conuri, in the very locality which his exploits and betrayal have made so famous. The accompanying inscription, in Roman mixed minuscules, seems to spell *Fecununi*. There is a vertical dash over what has been taken for the *c*, which may affect the reading. One cannot help suspecting that it is a *t* inverted, and that the reading is—

Fect Cununi.

"the tomb of Cunun," recalling the *conuneatt* of the main legend.

73. We have thus travelled through a country more thickly enriched with Ogham remains than any other district of equal extent elsewhere; and perhaps it may be a relief to look northward and eastward as far as the eye can reach from the summit of Slieve Mish, and learn that throughout all North Kerry, Limerick, Tipperary, and even beyond the visible horizon in Queen's County, King's County, Longford, Leitrim, and Westmeath, no Ogham legend is known to exist; nor has any been heard of, save, by doubtful report, near Tarbert, in North Kerry, and at Rathkeale and Knockfierna, in Limerick, respectively. If, indeed, we looked down in the opposite direction on the plain of Magonihy, the old Moy O'Conqin, the site of Ptolemy's Concani, extending southward from Slieve Mish to the Recks, we should contemplate a field of abundant material for such matter as has occupied us up to the present. To this field we shall return in completing the

circuit of the island which is now before us, and which will KERRY,
be made "desiul" with the left hand to the sea. And here, LIMERICK, CLARE.
in the northern boundary of the Oghamic district of Corkaguiny, it will not be out of place to observe that we are on
the dividing line between those parts of Ireland which Saint
Patrick is recorded to have visited, and the regions lying
south of the Galtee and Knockmeldown mountains from
hence to the confluence of the Suir and Barrow, into which
no apostle of the Patrician name appears, at any time, to
have penetrated.

74. I have referred to an inscribed stone near Tarbert, in
North Kerry. From Mr. Windele's drawing of it I would
suppose it to be one of the Ogham monuments now in the
Lane Fox collection in London. It is imperfect, but seems to
yield the name

BABROCI.
Babroci.

75. Of the example from near Rathkeale, in Limerick, I LIMERICK.
have no trace; but a drawing by Mr. Windele of the Knockfierna example has been preserved by Mr. Brash (Og. Mon.,
293), and is here copied from his work—

d qma maqi bogagaffecc.

The *maqi* determines the course of reading, and the *bogagaffecc*
following—however uncouth-looking—will be found to have
its substantial counterpart in other legends better authenti-
cated, to be hereafter noticed.

76. In North Limerick, at Adare, the Earl of Dunraven
has assembled a collection of Ogham monuments at Adare
Manor, the description of which ought properly to be in
connection with their places of origin. One, drawn by Mr.
Du Noyer (Lib. R.I.A.), reads, up one side, round the head,
and down the opposite side, without change of position,

Corbagni maqi bifiti.

Another will be found under Gortmacaree, further on.

77. Northward of the Shannon, in Clare, we hear of CLARE.
only one Oghamic inscription, but this is a monument in
many ways worthy of note. The south-west of Clare, and
up the wide alluvial valley of the Fergus as far as the

CLARE.

county town, Ennis, is a well-tilled country. Between Ennis and the sea the character of the scene changes, and near Miltown Malbay becomes rough and mountainous. Slieve Callan, the highest eminence in this tract, though not a lofty mountain, is a conspicuous feature from great distances all round. The leading road from Ennis westward traverses it at nearly its greatest height, having the summit and a little mountain tarn on the right hand. On one slope of the ridge, rising from the lake, stands a fine cromlech ; on the opposite slope, further from the road on the peaty, heathy surface,

Mount Callan
31
l. r.

lies the much-discussed Mount Callan inscription. It is a flagstone of about 9 ft. by 2½ ft., fractured at one end, and bearing an Ogham legend which at once strikes the eye as belonging to a school of inscriptional work different from anything we have so far observed, and strongly recalling the

Scholastic Ogham
13

style and appearance of what may be called the Scholastic Oghams of the books. Examples of these are found in manuscripts ranging from the ninth to the seventeenth century. Their characteristics are, a pen-drawn stem line, and vertical stem-crossing vowels as distinguished from oblique stem-crossing consonants. They are generally trivial notes or aphorisms designed, one would say, for the purpose of showing off the scribe's accomplishment. Thus in a MS. of the Annals of Innisfallen, in the Bodleian Library, we read—

Nemun (for nemo) sine numo honoratur nullus amatur.

> None without money honored ; yea, and none
> Loved, but has got some money of his own.

And in a British Museum MS. of the Brehon Laws—

> *Beithmaidne mar cach ais a locht*
> *So tis fom cosaib ba hi an comairchi.*

> As other ages ours : you, people, go
> Under my feet : have law's protection so.

But the series of characters, however long, is still, like all the

Words divided in *Callan* inscription and vowels stem-crossing.

legends we have yet noticed, without any kind of word-division. Here on the Callan Monument not only are the words divided by points over and under an incised stem-line, and all the vowels formed by stem-crossing digits, but the

whole legend is set in an incised frame or cartouche, giving Clare.
at first sight to those acquainted only with ordinary Ogham
an unexampled and questionable aspect. But Irish antiquaries, familiar with the word-separations of Scottish Ogham
legends, no longer look on these points with suspicion ; and the
surmises of fraud and forgery which at one time discredited
this monument may now be regarded as altogether displaced.
What chiefly excited the disposition to question its genuineness was an ambitious attempt of an Irish scholar patronised
by General Vallancey, Theophilus O'Flanagan, to translate
it in fourfold sequence, so as to produce, in modern Irish, a
sense appropriate to sepulchral commemoration whether read
from left to right or *vice versa,* or from one side of the stem-
line or the other. Besides, he made it the epitaph of Conan
Maoil, the contemporary of Finn Mac Coole, although, indeed,
he did not find the name Conan there, but only Collas or Conas,
which he took as Conaf ; and in his fourfold exposition, had not
only to supplement some digits and retrench others, but was
obliged, after his first *excursus* from left to right, to altogether
disregard the limitations of the word-divisions, refusing—as
they did—to fall in with his new syllabic necessities ; so that
when it was suggested that he himself had forged the inscription to play on the credulity of his patron, men's common sense
at once perceived the incongruity of a forger devising a fabricated text which would not lend itself to the exigencies of his
intended elucidation. But in truth no one can look on the
faint, weather-worn digits, hardly distinguishable from the
wrinkled surface on which they have been picked out, without
a strong persuasion that the inscription is many centuries old,
and, of whatever age, a genuine piece of work. But its tenor
is quite different from that of any other Oghamic sepulchral
legend. The word-divisions indicate the necessary course of
reading. If they be observed, the transliteration will run—

Fan : lia : do lica : co$^{s}_{ll}$as : colgac : cos : obad——

" Beneath this stone," although a formula foreign to
Oghamic sepulchral language, need not necessarily be more
modern than the " *sub hoc congeries lapidum*" of the Carausius
monument in Wales, adjudged by competent scholars to some

time before the eighth century. I presume that *do lica* means
" jacet," though I am unable to explain the use of the sign of
the past tense; which is hard to reconcile with monumental
language. No such name as Conas, so far as I know, is found
in Irish nomenclature. Even were it Conan Maoil, as the country
people have always assumed it to be, the excessive antiquity
demanded would be discredited by the modern aspect of the
legend. One conjecture may reconcile us to these dis-
crepancies, and that is that the true reading may lie hid under
some of the cypher systems contained in the books which
have evidently supplied the form of the characters and the
style of their arrangement; but, as yet, no success· has
attended the effort to extract by such means anything more
intelligible than that rendering which *prima facie* presents
itself, however suspicious its appearance, " under this stone
lies Collas (or Cosas) (the) sword-accomplished, the (fleet)
footed."

78. Whatever be the nature or interpretation of the Mount
Callan inscription, no question of forgery can arise respecting
a memorial pillar on the summit of the eminence called
Knockastoolery, near Doolen Bay, on the coast road from
Lisdoonvarna, in the north of the same county: but the cha-
racters, though, I think, Oghamic, are illegible.

79. Neither has Galway, the next county to the north, nor
South Mayo, anything in the Ogham kind legible, though
traces, I am told, exist at Ross Hill, near Cong, and on the
" long stone " at Kilmaine, near Ballinrobe.

80. If we cross the Shannon, however, out of Galway eastward, we come, at Clonmacnois, in the King's County, on the
left bank of the river, on an unimpeached legend of what I
have called the Scholastic variety of Ogham. It is a little
flagstone bearing the name *Colman* in Roman letters, with
the annexed digits, to be read backwards :—

$$\text{III} \quad \text{I} \quad \text{IIII} \;_{\text{I-I}}\;\overline{\underset{\text{I}}{}}$$

That is " Colman *bocht* " or Colman *pauper*, a designation of
humility quite consistent with what we have seen in Kerry,
but, so far as being in Ogham, not countenanced by any of
the other numerous inscribed monuments found at Clonmac-

nois, these being exclusively in the Roman character, and
in the usual and regular sepulchral formula of the Irish
Patrician, as of the Scottish Columban Church, *Oroit do* or
Bendaci do, " a prayer for " or " a blessing on " the deceased.
There is nothing of this kind in Ogham, unless the *anm*, which
is found in about a dozen instances, stand for *anima*, and
imply a prayer for the soul. The distinction in the vast
number of cases is absolute and, as between Christians,
imports the existence either of independent or, what seems
more probable, of successive organisations.

81. As regards Colman *Bocht*, let me notice something
which is calculated to mislead, in old Irish written references
to Ogham. The word, as used, seems equally applicable to
an Ogham, a Rune, or any monumental *titulus.* Thus, Corc,
son of Lugaidh, banished from Munster, seeking shelter with
Feradach, King of Alba, bears letters of Bellerophon inscribed
on his shield in Ogham, " If the bearer come by day, cut off
his head before night; if he come by night, cut off his head
before day." The King of Lochlann brings to Ireland an
Ogham in the hilt of his sword, obviously a Rune. The nobles
and clerics of *Leth Quin* (Con's half of Ireland) are interred at
Clonmacnois—

> The nobles of the Clann Cuin lie
> Beneath the flagged, brown, sloping cemetery,
> A knot or branch over each body,
> And an accurate Ogham name.

Where what is meant is obviously a Roman-letter-written
name; for of the inscribed tombstones from Clonmacnois,
collected by Petrie, and edited with a care and learning not
unworthy of his name by Miss Stokes, not one, save this of
Colman Bocht, exhibits any trace of Ogham influence; but
all are inscribed in the same Hiberno-Roman character, of
which the Kilmalkedar alphabet stone may be taken as one
of the earliest examples.

82. Leaving this famous seat of the Patrician Christianity
of Leth Quin, with its round towers, sculptured crosses, and
elegantly inscribed little flagstones—for every personal
memorial of its dead shows forth the humility which we may

believe adorned them living,—let us ascend and, recrossing the Shannon into Roscommon, proceed towards what Ptolemy has designated the "other Royal town" of the island, which may with reasonable certainty be taken to be at Rathcroghan. The earthworks of this old residence of the Connaught Provincial Kings still stand ten miles south from Elphin, in the centre of the vast tract of grass land stretching from Boyle to Castlereagh. As Emania, the first "Regia" of Ptolemy, the remains of which still exist near Armagh, was the residence of the Ulster Kings and of Conor Mac Nessa, the most famous sovereign of their line, so Rathcroghan was the seat of Conor's divorced Queen, Meave, and her second-taken husband Ailill, King of the Olnegmacht, in whom we may without much difficulty recognise Ptolemy's Nagnatæ, or, as in another and probably a better manuscript of his geography, Nagmatæ. We are here in one focus of the great cycle of heroic story which revolves around Conor and Meave, and preserves the renown of Cuchullin, Conall Carnach, Ferdiad, and the other champions of the two provinces who fought in their wars. We can hardly doubt that such persons existed; and certainly barbaric history presents no better marked characters than Conor and Meave: he, learned, valiant, astute, amorous, cruel, unscrupulous: she, ambitious, magnificent, reckless in the pursuit of power and vengeance. Her name still lives in the topography of the country, although contemporary in the annals with that of Augustus. It is impossible to walk over the green plain about the Rath which she inhabited without being transported in imagination to these ancient times, and among the actors in her war with Conor which forms the subject of the great Irish epic, the *Tain bo Cuailnge.* The circular stone wall surrounding the *Relig na ree,* or royal cemetery, where the Pagan Connacian kings and nobles lie interred, is still traceable. About 30 yards westward is a smaller disused and churchless cemetery, also circular, within the area of which are the entrances to what is traditionally known as "Queen Meave's treasure-house." It is a fissure in the limestone rock which runs westward about 50 yards outside the circular boundary, and here an identical name has been preserved in

Ogham. The roof of the cave is formed by long stones laid Roscommon.
across the top of the cleft, and covered by the grassy surface.
A lintel over the direct entrance, which opens to the east, is *Rathcroghan*
Ogham-inscribed.   It exhibits an example of one of the (A)
subsidiary group of diphthongal forms not included in the
original Ogham paradigm.   This is the under-line curve
standing for *ui*, and possibly for *u* in its other vowel combi- 6.
nations.   All the characters are well cut, but whether the
terminal group is meant as three digits on, or under, the natural
stem line formed by the convexity of the stone, is uncertain.
If *on*, it is *u*, and the legend will read—

$$\text{QRAGUISM}_\text{F}^\text{U}$$

Qraguismu,

if *under*—

Qraguismf,

when probably *Qragui* may detach itself as a proper name, and
the rest of the legend remain to be regarded as a *siglum* or 152.
monogram not yet interpretable.

83. The entrance to the cave from the south offers some- *Rathcroghan*
thing more definite and of extreme interest.   The lintel, which (B)
crosses it at the line of junction with the other approach, bears
on its outer arris a name beginning with FR and ending CCI
with six vowel points between.   There is nothing to indicate
how these vowel equivalents are to be divided.   They are
capable of very numerous combinations, but the associated 10.
consonants suggest the most probable reading—

Fraicci

or

Freocci,

Fraic or *Freoc* being a proper name, which in the *Tain bo
Fraich* has local associations with Rathcroghan.

84. The legend on the inner arris is even more remarkable—

MAQIMEDFFI
Maqi Medffi.

The over-line digits forming the D and the under-line digits
forming the first F are in some degree apposited, and might 13.
be taken as GB,

Megbfi,

but I make no doubt but this slight overlap indicates no real modification of the text, and that the first reading is the true one. The name of Medff, here in her own peculiar crypt, is even harder to dissociate from an historical identity than was that of Conuri read under the shadow of Cahir Conree. But, if it be indeed the name of the Amazonian queen, there is nothing to tell us how long after her death it may have been borne by others, and like some other vocables already noticed, Medff may be masculine as well as feminine. We are impressed, perhaps awe-struck, with the possible presence of a memorial of the Helen and Semiramis of Irish epic romance, but I must be content to leave Rathcroghan with a sceptical mind, knowing what awaits us at the tomb of another queen later in date. It may help to some more definite idea of the uses of many caves which have and will come under notice, to refer to a statement in several of the Lives of Saint Patrick, regarding a subterranean apartment in the district beyond Boyle, on the borders of Sligo. He had need for vessels for his office, and, prompted by a dream, at a place not identified, called Slieve Grada, or " Orders Hill," found a cave, and in it an altar, and on the altar four glass chalices, with which he served his occasion.

85. With one exception, from Rathcroghan to the Atlantic, throughout southern and central Mayo, there appear to be no remains of any Ogham monument. Proceeding westward into the northern parts of Mayo, one reaches, at five miles beyond Killala, the village of Mullaghnacross, within a short distance of which, on the lands of Breastagh, stands a very fine Ogham-inscribed pillar. Its dimensions are nearly 12 ft. by $2\frac{1}{2}$ ft. by 2 ft. Two of its arrises have originally been occupied by Ogham lettering : part of the inscription on one being buried in the earth when the stone was set upright. What is chiefly remarkable, as regards its situation, is its great distance from other monuments of the Ogham class, and the singularly Patrician character of its local surroundings. It is on the immediate confines of the district of Foghill, the site of the wood of *Focluth*, from which St. Patrick, in his dream, thought he heard the voices of the Irish calling him to his mission. In the immediate vicinity is Rathban, a

residence of that Auley son of Fiachra, the contemporary and MAYO,
convert of Patrick, from whom the barony takes its name, FERMANAGH.
Fiersad Tresi, in which Tresi wife of Auley was drowned;
Ross-Erc, the foundation of his daughter *Serc*; Kilcummin,
that of his grandson Cummin Foda; and Dunfinne, the scene
of the capture of the murderers of his grandnephew Bishop
Ceallagh, are all within a radius of six miles. Auley's name
is variously spelled Amalgaid, Amolugid, and Amlongad. In
the last form it appears to survive on the Breastagh pillar.
The inscription purports to commemorate some descendant of
a Coirbre, son of Auley. The early part of it, occupying the
western arris, is defective at both beginning and end. If read
upward normally from the right, it yields—

✻ ✻ SDULENGESCAD ✻

In another reading downward the word ENGEL emerges; but
there is nothing definite to guide the course of the transliteration. On the opposite or northern arris of this face of the
pillar a clue exists in a distinct *maq*—

MAQCORRᏴRIMAQAMMLLO[NGI]TT
Maq Corrbri Maq Ammllo[ngi]tt.

86. Sligo, also, if one group of two or three characters on
Church Island in Lough Gill be excepted, has no Oghams.
Neither are such inscriptions known in Longford or Leitrim;
but bounding these counties on the north, Fermanagh FERMANAGH.
possesses several. These all lie to the north of Lough Erne
on the side of Tyrone. For the discovery of them we are
indebted to Mr. Wakeman, a worthy pupil in Irish archæology
of his former master, Petrie. In a sepulchral cairn on Topped *Topped*
Mountain, exhibiting no trace of Christianity beyond a ques- 23
tionable cross incised on one of its loose stones, he found the *u. l.*
legend—

Nettacu,

which may decide us to regard the *Netta* rather as the component of a proper name than as an independent vocable.
Another fine pillar observed by Mr. Wakeman near the Irvines-
town Station on the railway to Ballyshannon, had the ill fate
to be dressed for inspection by a stonecutter, whose restored
digits cannot be relied on.

87. Further north, a cromlech at Castlederg, in Tyrone, was some time ago an object of much antiquarian interest, not as exhibiting Oghams of the kind we have been examining, but as presenting one of the very few examples of incised scorings hitherto found in that class of rude stone monuments. I say was, because I hear it has been destroyed by the farmer on whose land it stood. Fortunately a cast of the scorings exists, and a careful drawing of the structure as it stood. There can be no doubt that the scorings preceded the imposition of the cap-stone, but I do not think they could ever have had a phonetic significance. They belong, however, to a well-marked and widely-extended class of sculpturings, which may be designated *pseudo* Oghams, seemingly imitated from true Oghamic examples by persons ignorant of phonetic characters, but impressed with the value and mystery of writing.

88. A very fine and interesting monument of the true Ogham type, brought to light by Mr. Wakeman, stands at Aghascribba, near the centre of Tyrone, in that district of the country approached from Pomeroy. It is a high, rough, but not solitary region. At the time of the Ulster Plantation the native Irish expelled from the fertile lowlands of Tyrone were fain to take up their abode in these recesses of the Munter Loney mountains. Here they continue to speak their old native language, and preserve their traditional courtesy and friendly manners, under circumstances which might well have barbarised a people of less generous attributes. They look on their monuments with reverence not untinged with superstition. The Ogham-bearing pillar was, at one time, thrown down by the farmer on whose ground it stood. " He had the floods in his byre," they say, " within the week," and was glad to set it up again. The fairies, they tell you, make their cavalcades about the great standing-stone in the next field, and a deep and prolonged musical note is sometimes heard from the detached stone standing eastward of the circle, which they call *Crucan atha na boithie,* or the Mount of the Ford or Field of the Bothie, higher up the hill. This little circle seems the remains either of a cairn or of a stone-built Bothie or bee-hive cell. There is nothing on the inscribed

pillar to indicate whether it be a Christian or Pagan monu- TYRONE.
ment. All that is legible of the legend is composed of over-
line characters—

DOTeCTaMQI * * * *

The under-line digits which expressed the patronymic, being
on the adjoining face exposed to the north, are almost wholly
obliterated and illegible. The name is not found in Irish
records so far as known to me, unless it be the Totect of the
Book of Invasions, where it is ascribed to one of a pre-
Milesian race, being, I would imagine, an earlier form of the
Tudida of Adamnan and *Toddadac* of the Dunbell Ogham.
The name Aghascribba seems to signify the Field of the
Writing, and presumably carries back the existence of the
monument to the first imposition of townland names—an
indefinite retrospect. To whatever age it may belong, one
cannot look around on the wide tracts of moor and craggy
waste intervening between its site and the nearest ecclesiastical
foundation (at Lower Bodoney, seven miles further down the
valley) without a sense of wonder at the art of writing having
so early penetrated into such a wilderness. Bodoney is the
Both domnach or *Domus dominica* of the Patrician establishment. *Both*, a house, is peculiar to this region. as Bovevagh
(Both Medhbha, the House of Meave), Boydafea (Both da
fiach, the House of the two Ravens), Raphoe (Rath-both, the
Fort-house); but, elsewhere through Ireland, the equivalent
word employed in similar compositions is Tech, *tectum.*

89. We are here near the watershed between Lough Foyle *Knock Many*
and Lough Neagh, and, returning southward over the high 59
u. l.
tableland of central Tyrone, come at its verge on the head-
waters of the Blackwater River, running into the latter basin.
The valley of the upper Blackwater, about Augher and
Clogher, known locally in Irish records as the Clossagh, is a
fertile and beautiful region, sheltered on the north by a
range of mountain, one outlying eminence of which overlooking the rich tract about Augher, interposes between that
plain and the secluded valley where Carleton, our Irish Ettrick
Shepherd, was born and educated. This is Knock Many, so
called as being the Hill of Bani, wife of Teuthal Techtmar and
mother of Felimy Rechtmar, royal names familiar in the

pedigrees of all the great Highland and Island families of Scotland. It was in Scotland Teuthal spent his early manhood during his exile, consequent on the Attacottic rebellion, when the unfree or tributary tribes (*Aitheach Tuatha*) revolted against their Milesian or Scotic conquerors. In Scotland probably he married Bani, daughter of a king, it is said, of Finland. Assembling his forces here, Teuthal returned to Ireland, where, after making great havoc of the servile tribes, he reinstated himself securely on the throne, and in the year of our era 111, if we may accept the testimony of our Annals, lost his queen who, it is added, on the same authority, was buried on Knock Many, in the Clossagh. The sides of the mountain are thickly wooded; the summit is bare, and on the summit are the remains of a great sepulchral tumulus of several chambers, still partly covered by the remains of their cairn, but for the most part open to the sky. The stones of one of these chambers only remain. Two of them are covered with barbaric designs of the same general style and character as that at New Grange and the monuments on the Boyne and at Slieve-na-Calliagh, another great assemblage of sepulchral tumuli near Oldcastle, on the borders of Meath and Cavan.

90. The general feeling of all these efforts at sculptural decoration is the same, and they all have a striking resemblance to the ornamentation seen in the Mani-Nelud and Gavr-inis monuments in Brittany. On the eastern flanking stone of the principal cell these concentric rings and parallel zig-zags exhibit a certain degree of regularity. Undulating lines form part of what looks like a work having some significance. Groups of these in definite numbers flow parallel to one another from other lines on which they abut. Other groups of straight lines stand on or depend from these. The whole aspect of the sculpture gives the idea of some kind of writing invested in a masquerade of barbaric flourishes and *bizarreries*. The same idea is conveyed by straight digit-like indentations cut across the edge of a walling slab at the opposite side, which recall at first sight very vividly one Ogham-like species of Rune. The Rune, it will be remembered, is either ordinary alphabetic, or cryptic, Rune.

The cryptic Rune may be indicated, either by branched stems, TYRONE. or by longer and shorter digits arranged across a band; the shorter ones indicating the *ait* or category to which the letter belongs, the longer ones its sub-number in the *ait*.

If it could be said that the digits which cross the band formed by the edge of the slab, here, had definite distinctions in length or otherwise, we would look with the keenest interest for the three of one kind and the two of the other which should yield us the B of Bani; but if Bani's name be here, it is concealed under some other device; for the lines are only nine in number, and are too obscure in their terminations to enable one to say whether they vary in length or otherwise on any system. They look like a pseudo-Rune, just as the flourished lines with which they are associated look like pseudo-Oghams imitated without understanding, as we see the straight strokes surrounding the head in a northern bracteate representing the Byzantine name illegible to the artist. If, then, this be the tomb of Bani, which, on the evidence, we can hardly doubt, we must either conclude that at the beginning of the second century, an ordinary Ogham legend was not procurable even for the wife of the monarch, or else that the ordinary Ogham was in her case elaborated and invested with æsthetical mystery, just as we see plain writing disguised in our own days in the affected alphabetic singularities of addresses and architectural plans. Our minds, however, will be better not made up to either conclusion till the whole subject shall have undergone a much fuller examination, and at more competent hands than mine.

CHAPTER IV.

Armagh, chief seat of the Patrician church—Inscribed dolmen at Lennan—Mulloch Ogham—Sepulchral cairns at Slieve-na-Calliagh, Tailten the Irish Olympia, celebrated for its games, &c.—The Boyne tumuli; New Grange—Castletimon Ogham—Donard; one of the three Christian churches founded by Palladius A.D. 430-1—Killeen Cormac: its connection with Duftach Macculugar, companion of St. Patrick: the burying place of his sept—The Hy-Lugair and Hy-Cormaic, descendants of Cucorb, King of Leinster, slain A D. 119—Ogham-inscribed stones at Killeen Cormac, Gowran, Claragh, Dunbell, Ballyboodan, Windgap, Ballyvooney, Island, Drumlohan; cave under its Killeen containing several Ogham legends—Kilgrovan—Ardmore; its Round Tower—Saint Declan's Bed, his pedigree

ARMAGH, MONAGHAN.

91. WITH the exception of some doubtful scorings at Corrody, in the County of Derry, and Mr. Wakeman's report of a supposed Ogham cave in Donegal, I know of nothing Oghamic in the northern parts of Ulster. But the neighbourhood of Armagh, the chief place of the Patrician church, furnishes one example. It comes from the vicinity of Pagan Emania, but bears a cross, described by Dr. Reeves, Bishop of Down and Connor.

MONAGHAN.

Lennan
19
u. c.

92. Southward from Armagh lies the County of Monaghan. In its hilly and rough division, to the north of Ballybay, in the parish of Tullycorbet, at a place called Lennan, we encounter a cromlech inscribed with characters. They are not indeterminate scorings as at Castlederg, but characters, some of which look like Runes, and one which resembles a Scholastic variety of Ogham. They were regarded by O'Donovan, when he examined the monument in 1834, as a forgery. I do not think that opinion will be entertained after an inspection of the cast. O'Donovan failed to observe a very significant sculpture above these characters. It looks like a galley, as galleys are represented on the sculptured monuments of Brittany and Scandinavia. Save the scorings on this and the Castlederg cromlech, and channel-like indentations on the upper side of the covering stone at Brennanstown, near Dublin, I know of no other inscribed dolmens in MONAGHAN, Ireland. CAVAN, MEATH, CAVAN.

93. Where the hilly country of Monaghan and Cavan subsides into the rich plain bordering Meath, we again meet with a regular Ogham at Mulloch, near Virginia Water. It *Mulloch* stands in the churchyard beside the parish church, and is *l. c.* legible up one arris—

OSBARR,

or, possibly, *Osbarrn*, a name looking to historic times, and, although unaccompanied by any Christian symbol, very unlikely to be Pagan.

94. Advancing into Meath, a line of green bare heights MEATH. rising from the wooded plain is visible along the western boundary of the valley of the Blackwater. For a distance of two miles these Slieve-na-Calliagh hills, as they are called, consti- *Slieve-na-* tute a vast cemetery of scattered sepulchral cairns. The group *Calliagh* reaches to within eight miles of that part of the Blackwater *c.* where Telltown is at this day thought to preserve the name and site of Taltin, the old Irish Olympia, famous for its triennial fairs, races, and games, and celebrated also as one of the great cemeteries of the country "before the faith." Hence it has been supposed that in these Slieve-na-Calliagh cairns we have the remains of Irish Pagan interments; and they do, in all respects, present an appearance in accordance with that idea. The cairn contains its central domed chamber, approached by a narrow adit, as at Maeshow or New Grange on the Boyne. The chamber is the vestibule to inner cells, on whose floors rest shallow stone sarcophagi. The walls and roofing slabs are covered with carved devices, more wild and fantastic even than those of the Bani monument. Circles, zig-zags, pittings, fringes of straight lines, maggot-like objects, and others somewhat resembling boats with vertical lines for the crews, are scattered over the surface, apparently without design or connection. The nearest resemblance found to these freaks of the graver, out of Ireland, is on the Coilsford stone in Ayrshire. A possible chariot preceded by a diapered fantasy which may have been intended for horses, is one of the few instances of an apparent attempt at representation of any known object. The only exception

F

to this fantastic sort of figuring is found on the lintel of the southern cell of the central cairn. Here are what have very generally been supposed to be Ogham digits, some of them crossing the arris; but the greater number on the flat, and independent of that or any other stem-line. They much resemble the Knock Many scorings. They have all the appearance of being contemporaneous. They have, no doubt, a purpose, and, possibly, a phonetic meaning. Certainly, if the Ogham be a development of any earlier system, we are here among its roots and first manifestations, and the nature of that other system, if it existed, will have to be investigated on the assumption that some relation holds between these figures and the numbers of their lines, and the undiscovered *aicmes* and sub-numbers of some primitive alphabet.

Ornamentation on bone objects found in caves. **95.** In these cairns have been found considerable collections of bone objects, some of which bear incised designs of interlaced ornamentation, as if intended as matrices for metal-work. Were we to accept these as records of the builders, we should conclude that the fantastic figuring of the cell walls was executed by those who could have covered them with elegant and regular pattern work if they had pleased, but who adopted the barbaric design, or seeming want of design, as something perhaps traditionary and possibly hieratic. The same may be said of most of the caves which have yielded engraved bones elsewhere. The etchings on the bones contrast strongly with the barbarous rudeness of their surroundings. I see no way of escaping the conclusion that a higher art co-existed with the use of traditionary barbarisms in sepulchral monuments, unless we suppose these rifled cairns and tumuli to have been used as hiding-places and workshops by Wayland Smiths of a later period; and, in this view, it may be worth remarking that in Irish tradition such caves are regarded as the haunts of musicians and artificers of the old Tuatha de Danaan race, who first brought in the knowledge of the arts, and, on their conquest by the Milesians, hid themselves underground.

96. From the Slieve-na-Calliagh cairns to those of the Boyne is a distance of about twenty miles. The Boyne tumuli and their chambers are too well known to require any lengthened description. I would but call attention to the sculpturing *Meath, Dublin, Wicklow.* of a slab from New Grange, which it will be seen offers in its general design a great similarity to the Bani monument. *New Grange* 19 *l. r.* There are the same flowing zig-zags and concentric circles, but none of the wilder grotesques, either of the Bani stone or of the intermediate group. It would be hard to conceive of anything phonetic lying hid under these forms. One device, however, does exist on the headstone of the western cell at New Grange, which certainly has a monogrammatic and in some degree an Oghamic appearance. It will recall very vividly the discontinuous cross lines of the Tyvoria example. It can hardly be but that, after what has been seen, some systematic examination of these devices on the Irish Pagan monuments of Tyrone and Meath will be undertaken by competent observers, who may be able to say definitively whether these are merely insensible ornamentation or phonetic elements fantastically disguised. Any traces Meath may retain are, I believe, illegible, or *quasi* Oghamic.

97. Neither does Dublin, save in one illegible example at *Dublin.* Portmarnock, afford local examples. Those assembled at the *Portmarnock* 15 *u. c.* Royal Irish Academy have been in part, and will be, for the remainder, noticed in connection with their places of origin, so far as these can now be ascertained. There are two of them which I have been unable to ascertain whence they come, further than that I believe them to be from Kerry, probably sent up by Mr. Hitchcock. Lest this supposition should be erroneous, I think it better to notice them here. The first presents another example of the name *Gusacht,* already noticed; it is an old and well-known name in Irish hagiology. The first bishop of Ardagh was Gusact son of Milchu, Saint Patrick's pagan bondmaster. The inscription is well preserved and complete. Its difficulties arise from the absence of the usual *Maqi,* or perhaps from the absence of *Maqi* in its usual spelling—

$$\text{GOS}^{U}_{O}\text{CT}^{I}_{EA}\text{SMOSACMA}\overset{P}{\widetilde{FA}}\text{INI}$$
&c

The word-division will depend on whether *Gosucti* be taken as the genitive, or *Gosucteas,* which is more in accordance with the Corkaguiny example. If the first, we have *Gosucti smosac*, seemingly a term of humiliation, followed by *mapi* (the equivalent of *Maqi*) *Ni*. *Maqini* and *Maqi Ne* are found elsewhere, *Ni* being apparently the genitive of the name *No*, also found further on. If read *Gosucteas*, the second name should be taken as one of the numerous class formed in *mo*, "my," probably *Mosocma*. Grounds have been thought to exist for reading this *Mosocra*, the name of a saint in Irish hagiology; but I think there has been a mistake of fact. If read either of the latter ways, the X character should not be taken as a vocable, and the residue be read as *ini*, "here." It seems to me that fewer difficulties attend the reading first suggested—

Gosucti smosac mapi Ni.

The stone of " Gusact MUCOSUS son of No."

Conf.   *Spumosus* (   ).

The second Academy stone of uncertain origin bears the legend—

$$\text{MUCOTU}^{\text{DD}}_{\text{C}}\text{A}^{\text{DD}}_{\text{C}}\text{AC}$$

where the resemblance of the vocables Tuddaddac to a proper name found on one of the Kilkenny monuments, noticed further on, seems to detach *Muco* as possibly an equivalent of *Maqi* in some secondary stage of filiation,—a matter worthy of consideration in connection with *Mucoi*. I do not take *Mu* as equivalent to the " mo " of *Mocatoc*, whose name has been thought to be recorded here.

98. Wicklow County now takes up the chain of connection, the links of which will become closer as we return towards the south. At Castletimon, in Dunganstown parish, between the remains of a cromlech and the sea, at the side of the high road, lies a large boulder-like block, which may have better served the purpose of a coped grave-stone than a pillar monument, bearing very legibly along its rounded arris—

NETACARINETACAGNI.

What will first strike us is that here are two names conceived in the A's B formula, and that *neta* enters as a component into both, like the *netta* of earlier observed examples.

"Netacar's Netacag" has certainly an odd aspect, and WICKLOW. induces a suspicion that some other name is concealed under adventitious syllables, as in the *formolad* process already referred to. *Carantoc* would be the name most likely to be so hidden, and *neta* merely a suffarcination and disguise.

99. Behind us, in the mountain country dividing Wicklow *Glendalough* from Kildare, are the ruins of St. Kevin's ecclesiastical City of 23 Glendalough, another centre of Patrician teaching and dis- *u. r.* cipline; but neither here do we find any trace of Oghamic writing.

100. If we cross the mountain, however, towards Kildare, *Donard* and descend on Donard, lying at its western base, we are 21 again in a well-marked Ogham district, including the remark- *u. r.* able cemetery of Killeen Cormac, which contains four examples. In the stone fences about Donard fragments of Ogham monu- ments are numerous, and the names of the farmers who broke them up are remembered. A short mile from the village on the south-west stands the Ogham-inscribed pillar called the Piper's Stone. The common tradition of profane dancers *Piper's stone.* and musicians being turned into stone exists here as in most other districts abounding in stone monuments. The Piper's Stone is excessively rugged, and its legend most difficult to decipher. It shows the X character, and seems to read—

INIGI.

101. Donard is and always has been accepted as one of the three Christian churches founded by Palladius during his short mission to the Irish in A.D. 430-1. The authority is of vene- rable, not to say respectable, antiquity. The three churches designated are—Killfinte, Tech na Romanach, and Domnach Arda. Killfinte has, on plausible grounds, been supposed to be Killeen Cormac. There is no question that the House of the Romans is the present Tigroney, near Wicklow, nor that Domnach Arda—*Dominica domus alta*—is Donard. Although Tigroney offers no Ogham remains, yet their existence at the other two sites must detract from the force of what has previously been said respecting their absence from Glen- dalough and the other seats of that Patrician Christianity which followed on the mission of Palladius. It is more pro- bable, however, that the Ogham use spread hither from a

KILDARE

*Killeen
Cormac*
32
l r.

centre further south, towards which its evidences extend in an unbroken connection and increasing numbers from hence to the great Oghamic tract of South Munster.

102. Killeen Cormac lies beyond Dunlavin, six miles to the west, in the lands of Cobbinstown, in a detached portion of the parish of Davidstown, in the County of Kildare. It is still used as a regular burial place, although without any remains of an associated church. It is a mound of considerable dimensions, piled up by successive interments from the ground level. Were the upper strata removed and the superficial sepulchral constructions laid bare, it would, judging from what can be seen of these round the under margin, present much the same appearance as a denuded cemetery of apparently the Pagan period near Glencolumkill, in the County of Donegal. Each interment is in its own stone-built cist, and these are of large dimensions. The entrances are seen to two such sepulchral *cellæ* of the second storey, if I may so say, of this exuvial edifice, divided by a stone-pillar, which bears traces of Ogham on its top, and has down each side a groove for the reception of the closing stone.

103. At the foot of this most ancient and remarkable grave mound, near the entrance to the level surrounding enclosure, lies a fine pillar-stone inscribed in Roman and in Ogham characters. There can be no question that the word "Druides" forms part of the Roman epigraph, and this being the only instance of the mention of Druids on any known lapidary monument anywhere, the double inscription cannot but be regarded with extraordinary interest. It seems to me to be in part at least bilingual and biliteral. The Roman epigraph may read—

IVVENEDRVIDES
Ivvene druides,

or, owing to a flaw making it doubtful if the fifth letter be R or N—

IVVEREDRVIDES
Ivvere druides,

or, by an allowable use of the two first characters in their numerical value—

IV (that is *Quatuor*) *vere druides.*

Thus, it may signify the stone of " the Druid Youths," or the KILDARE. stone " of Juvan the Druid " (for the *es* genitive need not, in view of the Welsh examples, embarrass us), or the stone " of the Four true Druids." At this stage let us examine the associated Ogham and see which construction it may favour. The obvious regular-marked digits read—

UFANOSAFIEFRATTOS.

Ufanosafiefrattos.

Taking it as *Ufano safi*, and considering that *saei* is the *Various read-* modern and middle Irish for sage, wise man, *sophos*, it *ings of the Ogham on* appears not an unlikely echo of Juvan the Druid. But where *JuveneDruides* is the J ? It has no regular equivalent in Ogham ; and we *stone.* may ask is not the *s* necessary to complete *Ufanos*, whether it be nominative or genitive ? If so, we should be left to utilise the second word as *afi*, accepting Stokes and Rhys's version of it as the early Celtic for " descendant of." Then we should enquire for the patronymic. The reading has hitherto been *Sahattos*, but the plaster cast taken from the paper mould shows distinctly, though faintly, what the stone itself, overshadowed by trees as it is, could never reveal, that the reading is *Efrattos* ; and " Ufan of the descendants of Efratt," would be a better sequence than " Ufan the sage," with " Efratt" standing by itself. But there are some scorings or characters, besides, which must also be taken into account. An imperfect *d*, not in parallelism with the vertical digits we have been discussing, precedes the *Ufan*. I call it imperfect because one digit is boldly and the other very slenderly incised, and over the last digit of the *f* a delicately carved very minute *t*, stands just above the line. Here the *Quatuor vere druides* reading begins to receive some countenance. As we omit or bring in these supernumerary characters, we may have Ufan or Dufan or Duftan, or were it allowable to take *n* for its opposite, Duftaq, and so the efforts of my learned friend, *Rev. J. Shear-* the Rev. Mr. Shearman, who has long laboured to connect *man connects Killeen* Killeen Cormac with Duftac Macculugar, the companion of *Cormac with* St. Patrick, would be rewarded. I cannot take upon me *Duftac Mac-culugar, com-* to do that violence to this text, though I am aware that *panion of St.* scholars of eminence do not shrink from such changes when *Patrick.* the exigencies of other inscriptions seem to require it. The minuscular *t* is a very small object, but not more minute than some Ogham characters, which I cannot decipher, occurring on a twin pillar lying beside. A very faint and rudely-outlined head of the Saviour is picked in on the upper face of this monument, and on the arris to the left these Oghams are incised. Whatever we may say of Duftac himself, the

Killeen Cormac connected with Duftach's sept of the Hy-Lugair. connection of the place with Duftach's sept of the Hy-Lugair, is well made out. The bounds of the sept, as laid down in the old Irish books, embrace it. It is the only topographical Killeen in the Diocese of Glendalough, and a *Killeen ulugair*, "on the other side of the mountain," is enumerated among the possessions of that see in A.D. 1183. Then, Duftach himself is recorded, with many other eminent ecclesiastics, to have been buried in the *dinnlacha* or marsh-hillocks of the Hy-Lugair, which, from the peculiarity of the position, can hardly mean any other place. Next, as regards

Cucorb, King of Leinster, slain A.D 119, ancestor of the Hy-Cormaic and Hy-Lugair. the name *Killeen Cormaic*. The Hy-Lugair were a branch of the Hy Cormaic, both septs being descendants of Cormac, son of Cucorb, King of Leinster, who was slain A.D. 119, by Felimy Rechtmar. Eighth in descent from this Cormac was Saint Abban, whose designation in old Irish genealogical description would be Maccu Cormaic. On the death of this holy person

Saint Abban : contention for his relics. a contention for his relics sprang up between the men of North Leinster where he died, and those of South Leinster, where he had chiefly ministered. The feud was composed by the appearance of two wains drawn by miraculously sent oxen— a common device in such cases,—each carrying the seeming remains of the saint, which, taking different directions, led the combatants off the field, and after the entombment, vanished in the fords of neighbouring rivers. Now, the local tradition at Killeen Cormaic is that the Cormac buried there, and from whom the place has its name, was a king whose remains were brought thither by certain oxen, which, after a hound accompanying them had indicated the spot for the entombment, by leaving the impress of his paw on the head of a standing-stone, went off and vanished in the River Greise. King Arthur's hound, which left the track of his paw in Buieth to serve as one of Nennius's wonders of Britain, may have suggested that part of the story relating to the dog's paw still

shown at the Killeen, but the rest of the tradition has such a KILDARE.
likeness to the story of the descendant of Cormac, son of
Cucorb, as may lead to the probable conclusion that his are
the obsequies referred to. Let it be observed further that the
son of Cormac, from whom the two tribes or *Finne* of the
Hy-Cormaic and the Hy-Lugair sprang, was Labraid, and in
reference to Labraid, which happens to correspond with the
third person singular of the present tense of *labraim*, " I
speak," let me recall the story of Labraid Longseach told *Story of*
by Keating. "Does the comer by sea (*Longseach*) speak ?" *Labraid Long-*
asked the druid of the supposed dumb exile, who had returned *seach.*
with his Gaulish auxiliaries to take vengeance on his enemies.
"Labraid"—he speaks—was the reply, and so Labraid, the
Speaker, the eloquent, became a noted name. If we have
rightly identified the hillocks in the Hy-Lugair marshes, it will
not be Duftach Maccu-Lugair, and Abban Maccu Cormaic
alone, whose sepulchres we may expect to find here, but those
also of several other eminent descendants of this Labraid;
including three sons of Duftach and a female saint of great
celebrity, Cuach or Coningen, all of whom are recorded to lie
together in the same "Dinnlacha." Supposing then, the true
reading to be *quatuor vere druides*, Mr. Shearman may be well
excused for his persistence in believing that at least under
their "Ogham names," if not ostensibly, Duftach himself and
some of the three others are not only interred here, but
monumentally commemorated in the inscription under consideration; for four persons being indicated, and *afi* taken as
meaning " descendant of," it is plain that the same descent,
from some one here called by his Ogham name of Efrattos, is
predicated for each of them; and *Efrattos*, it must be owned,
has all the appearance of a Greekish equivalent of *Labraid*,
the speaker. If this be so, we may see that whether the
reading be *Iuvene Druides*, reflected in the *Ufanos afi efrattos*
of the Ogham, or *Quatuor vere Druides* reflected in the
fourfold reading suggested by the supplemental and minuscular digits, it would be equally true of all to designate him
or them as *de nepotibus Labradii*.

104. But it will have occurred to you to ask, How could
these great grandsons of Labraid, who was but fourth in

KILDARE,
KILKENNY.

descent from Cucorb, have possibly lived in the fifth century? Abban was seventh only from Cucorb, which, at thirty years to the generation, places him (A.D. 119 + 210 = 329) more than a century before the commission of Palladius. It may be that some generations have dropped out of the pedigree; but if the discrepancy could have been explained on that suggestion, the old Irish hagiologists would not have had occasion to allege, as they do, that this Abban lived three hundred and sixteen years, being the time necessary from the presumable date of his birth to bring him into chronological conformity with the Annals. We stand, indeed, amazed at the vision of possible pre-Palladian times, which seems to rise before us in contemplating this mortuary hillock in the Hy-Lugair marshes.

*Killeen
Cormac
" decedda "
stone.*

105. Half way round the mount to the right of the "Druides" stone lies, or formerly lay, another displaced block, inscribed in Ogham round both arrises and the top—

MAQIDDFCCEDAMAQIMARIN.

Maqi ddecceda maqi Marin.

We recognise the *decedda*, but *Marin*, seemingly complete, is new, and, unless *n* be separable, not easily reconcilable to other forms.

106. Beyond the "decedda" stone half way round to the right, stands a pillar bearing digits in a new arrangement. Here one digit is made to serve as stem-line for others, in a kind of sub-virgular dependence, obviously contrived for cryptic purposes. Another example of the same device will occur further on. It seems to be a kind of *rebus* for *doftos*.

KILKENNY

Gowran
20
l r

107. Turning westward and southward from Killeen Cormac, we cross the rich garden of Carlow into the County of Kilkenny, where at Gowran Abbey we find another cross-signed flag-stone which has once borne a long Ogham legend, now much mutilated as well as the cross. The crutched heads of the arms of the cross have been chipped off, as it would seem, to form the arrises on which the remains of the Ogham text are found, an apparent evidence of the prior existence of the cross, quite contrary to what has often been advanced regarding the supposed earlier inscription of the Ogham in such cases. The frequent *Maqi Mucoi* is recognisable on one arris.

On the other, remains of what may have been the name KILKENNY. Laserian in the inflated form—

LASICAREIGNI.

108. At Tulloherin, in the same neighbourhood, distinct *Tulloherin* but illegible remains of another Ogham exist on a truncated 24 *l. c.* pillar near the base of the round tower in the parish grave-yard ; and at the ruined church of Claragh, built into the *Claragh* wall over the western doorway, a long stone is seen having 20 *u. c.* the legend—

TASEGAGNI MUCOI MAQR * * * *

the masonry concealing the rest of the patronymic. Here is " Mucoi " without a *maqi* preceding, used apparently as designating the status or character of Tascen, the person commemorated. Haigh's *mucoi*, " daughter," would suit the context, but so to conclude would be premature.

109. In the adjoining parish of Dunbell to the west there *Dunbell* are traces of excavations from which two very fine Ogham 20 *l. c.* pillars, now in the Museum of the Royal Historical and Archæological Association at Kilkenny, were extracted, many years ago. The site does not appear to have been ecclesiastical. The stones were broken in numerous fragments by the farmer for more convenient removal off the land, but were fortunately discovered by the Rev. James Graves and Mr. Prim, two active officers of the Society, in time to prevent their conversion to sordid uses. Reconstructed, by fitting their fragments together, they are both legible, and read—

$$\text{BRAN}^{E}_{I}\text{TT}^{A}_{O}\text{SMAQID}^{O}_{U}\text{CR}^{e}_{i}\text{DDA}$$

(recalling the possible " Dugreddos " of the Ballynahunt example), and

$$\text{SAFFIQEGITT}\,U^{DD}_{C}\text{ATTAC}$$

where the double *d* may be a *c*, and the name a form of *Toichthec*, as reflected in the Cahir-na-gat legend, where we read Togittacc. *Saffiqeg* seems a strange appellation, but we meet it again in its less dignified form *Sfaccuc*, still a very odd-sounding collocation of vocables, and suggestive of some trick of literal antithesis such as may have more than once occurred to our minds in other cases.

110. Ballyboodan, in Knocktopher parish, more to the south, has furnished its last acquisition to the Kilkenny Lapidary Museum. It is a fine pillar, still legible enough to show that it records the name of

Corbi poi maqi labridd (a).

" Corb, that was son of Labraid," the " *poi* " being expressed by ꭓ with its attendant vowels. Labrid may be of any antiquity, but *Corb*, " wicked," " lewd," " accursed," sounds in self-deprecation and savours of the cell. Another recent addition to the Kilkenny Museum is noticed by Mr. Atkinson. Not having seen it, I abstain from reproducing the suggested reading.

111. Crossing the Suir from Kilkenny through Tipperary into Waterford at Carrick-on-Suir, we have in front and on the right the rugged group of the Commeragh Mountains; on the left, the woods and far-spreading glades of Curraghmore. A road leading to Rathgormuc passes, at about two miles from Carrick, through the lands of Windgap, where in a cave in a circular earth fort, locally called Rath-Coolnamuck, a boldly cut flagstone preserves the legend—

MODDAGNI MAQI GATIGNI MUCOI LUGONI.

" Of Modan, son of Gatin Mucoi of Lugon." It may seem to you that it continues to favour the hypothesis of Haigh, that " mucoi " signifies daughter.

112. Taking the high road towards Curraghmore and Kilmacthomas, we come, at 3½ miles from Carrick, on a tract abounding in stone monuments at Ballyquin, where the great stone which appears to have borne the legend *Catabar moco firiqorrb* stands at the right side of the high-road, serving as a massive and lofty gate-post. There are few more imposing monuments, or more like what we might be inclined to suppose survivals from Pagan times, in Ireland. Cromlechs exist near it, and a double-chambered cave, probably sepulchral. Cromlechs, however, need not be regarded as all pre-Christian. At Ballina, in Mayo, the *lac na tri maoil* is a perfect cromlech though raised over persons put to death in the seventh century; and the *moco* of Cathbar's family name may appear to readers of Adamnan's life of Columba less antique than the WATERFORD more frequent *maqi*.

113. If we proceed southward from Kilmacthomas we reach *Ballyvooney* the sea coast near the picturesque little town of Stradbally. About half a mile to the east at Ballyvooney, in a secluded glen running down to the sea shore, is a holy well covered over by stone slabs, all sadly bemired and broken, but two of them bearing Ogham-inscribed names of novelty and interest. The first—

24
l c.

Netafroqi maqi qit.   (A)

The *qit*, as a proper name, need not revolt us. *Carn Kit* is the tomb of Cath, the slayer of Queen Meave in Roscommon. *Netafroq* may be readily recognised as Natfraic in its state dress. We continue to find *Neta* entering into name-composition, and begin to reconcile our minds to rejecting the idea of its being a separate vocable. The fragments of the second, put together, yield the epigraph,

Qrita ——o maqi lobat,   (B)

with the elegant associated names—

Afinia, Gracolini.

One naturally asks, Were these the names in religion of Qritt and Lobat respectively? and whence came the classical taste which so long ago brought these non-Celtic sounds into a pastoral recess of the Waterford sea-coast?

114. I must crave your patience to refer to some of the monuments of early Irish church history. The name of Ængus the Culdee, who flourished in the reign of Aid Ornighe, *Ængus the* A.D. 793 to 817, is known as that of the author of two very *Culdee.* venerable religious compositions—one, which has been edited by Dr. Whitley Stokes, a surprising monument of palæographic and philological accomplishment, as it is also a splendid example of literary purity and elegance in the use of our language, the Felire or Fasti of the Saints, especially *His " Felire,"* those of Ireland; and the other which still awaits the hand *edited by Dr.* *Whitley* of the modern scholar, his Litany, partly published by Petrie *Stokes.* in his Essay on Irish Ecclesiastical Architecture. In the Litany Ængus invokes various holy persons and companies of *His " Litany."*

WATERFORD. religious men and women, Romans, Italians, Gauls, Britons, Saxons, who had flocked to Ireland in primitive Christian times in search of the happiness afforded by the ascetic life. Doubtless we are here, at *Tubber Kill Eilte*, near the site of some Latin *cœnobium* of these early times, and truly no place could be found better fitted for a tranquil and contemplative life.

Island   **115.** Another remarkable legend exists at a place called Island, near the sea, on the opposite side of Stradbally. On one side of the stone is inscribed—

95   CUNETaSMA[Q]IGU$^{C}_{T}$

and on the other, reading upward—

Qomagecafec,

or, read reversely—

netasegemon.

I acknowledge my inability to determine which is right. We shall find an equally perplexing choice set before us in the principal inscription at Ardmore, of which presently.

Drumlohan   **116.** The rath-cave of Drumlohan is the next point to which
24   we shall proceed; but I must here speak from my own
c.   drawings, in which I recognise the same liability to error as in the drawings of others. Drumlohan lies two miles north from Stradbally, a rough boggy country, through which runs the drum or ridge of arable land giving it its name. Within a wide circular earthen fort, exists an entirely disused *Killeen*.

Killeen with cave. In removing part of the circular embankment, a cave was found extending under it and partaking of its curve. The stones forming the side walls and roof almost all bear Ogham legends, but, having been inscribed before they were turned to this use, have for the most part portions of their texts concealed. Imperfect, however, as many of them are, they introduce us to further new and characteristic local names, and possibly to something new in the monotonous vocabulary hitherto employed. The lintel stone over the entrance seems to me to read along one arris and round the head—

(A)   *manumagu nogati mo (coi),*

and along the opposite arris,

Macarb.

Mac Arb, we learn from the Brehon Laws, is the designation of one who has graduated in poetry.

117. The fourth roofing slab presents the name,

Drumlohan

Calunofiq maqi mucoi,

(B)

with following characters which Mr. Brash reads, I believe rightly, *litof,* so far as they are visible. We have here the first example of a class of early Munster names in *fic,* which we shall often meet with.

118. The sixth roofing slab on one arris has what I take to be the name in the nominative,

(C)

Lafic,

and on the other,

Maqini.

If Ni be the patronymic, we might suppose it to be the genitive of some such form as Na, which we shall meet with hereafter; and here again we find ourselves introduced to a monosyllabic nomenclature somewhat strange to the eye, but corroborated by many names of the like kind in the older records, such as Al, En, Un, Id, Ith, &c.

119. The seventh roofing stone is inscribed on all its angles. The cave being near the surface, it is easily stripped, and when exposed exhibits a continuous and nearly perfect legend—

(D)

Cunalegea maqi c (   ) l ar Celuufiq feci (o ?).

Remembering the *Qeniloci* of St. Manchan's, and the *Qeniloegni* of Martramane, we recognise the principal name which probably was in its local form Culoc or Cenlogha, son of someone whose name seems to have begun with C, and to have ended with l. We also have sufficient examples to familiarise us with *Celufic* as a personal name; but the particle "ar" between is new. "Ar,' whether in modern or ancient Irish, so far as my little knowledge extends, when used as a preposition means "on," "at," "for," and if this be its employment and meaning here, it is the first equivalent yet

WATERFORD. met with of the "at" and "after" of Runic sepulchral legends. Thorstein set this stone "at" his father Thorkill. Sweno let raise this stone "after" his mother. Such is the Norse epitaph in its simplest form. But it puts our Celtic "A son of B," or even this, "A son of B *for* C,"—as I take it, so far, to mean—to some discredit in point of expressiveness; and when it goes beyond the simple formula, though still concise, it is full, predicative, biographic, and even picturesque to an extent not matched by the epitaphs of any other people. If I have read the legend aright, another word of necessary significance to complete the statement remains after Culufic—*feci*, offering to us, if we be willing to accept a Latin formula in Irish company, the complete meaning: "I, Cunalegea, son . (or daughter, we may probably be disposed to say) of C., have made this for Celufic." Two faint indentations follow, which may be *o*. It would, perhaps, extend your complaisance too far were I to suggest *opus* or *officium*, although authority might be found for both, but in non-Celtic association. My reading, however, not being supported by a cast, must be taken for what it is worth, considering that Mr. Brash (275) has read the characters—

Cunalegea maqicetai desradcq feci.

120. The last legend exhibited by the cross-laid lintels of the roof yields the very archaic-looking names—

(E)
Igu maqi dag,

and I am unable at this time to say whether the text is complete, though I have no doubt it is rightly transliterated.

121. The wall stone to the left at the entrance has the legend—

(F)
Bir maqi mucoi rottais.

It may be Bir, son of "Mucoi" Rottais; but, if so, we have here a genitive in *ais* not countenanced by any other example. Bir is not found as a proper name in the books, so far as I know, although among such names as have been lately enumerated it need not be considered very singular. But *birrotais* has a meaning, and if found by itself would

readily, after what we have seen, be taken as a name of dis- WATERFORD.
paragement. Here again *Maqi Mucoi*, if not a step in pedigree, could not be other than an interjection.

122. The third walling stone is inscribed on the face—

Maqini. (G)

What may be at the back cannot be ascertained.

123. The fifth walling stone shows the names

Odafe maqi Denafe, (H)

both new, and for both of which I rely on the accuracy of
Mr. Brash.

124. On the right, or western, side of the cave is only one
inscription. It occurs on the block fifth from the entrance.
I read it

Digos maqi muco(i), (I)

with probably an unseen continuation behind.

125. That these stones have come ready inscribed from the
adjoining Killeen, or, as it is called in this part of the country,
Killeena, seems highly probable, but the construction of the
cave has exhausted the supply. Looking at the remains as
they exist, one would be disposed to say, The Killeen was
first, the encircling Rath next, and the Rath-cave made from
the spoil of the dismantled cemetery.

Returning to the coast, as we approach Dungarvan, *Kilgrovan*
another deserted, but not wholly dismantled *Killeena* is 31
l. r.
reached at Kilgrovan. The place is open and arable. A
little spot is left untilled overlooking the sea. Four rude flagstones were here set up as pillars when I first visited it:
one only is standing now. The impression given is that
they have been brought together out of a larger area.
They are all inscribed. One bears excessively coarse and now
illegible indentations, but evidently Oghamic. Another
reads—

Olni mucoi cunuu. (A)

The third pillar bears the legend—

(B)

]NAMAQILUGUDECAMUCO[ı]MATONI.
Na maqi lugudeca muco (i) matoni.

145. If *na* be not like *No, per se* a proper name, Namaton might be taken to be the true *titulus* with the matter ending *mucoi* interjected. Lugudeca we shall find elsewhere as Lugudeccas in the genitive, an evidence either of the unfixed grammar used by the Ogham writers, or of linguistic changes implying long lapse of time.

(C)

126. The fourth Kilgrovan pillar offers some features giving rise to a consideration of more distinct interest. We have seen that the characters of the supplementary *aicme* in the Ogham alphabet stand for the respective vowels in their diphthongal combinations, as X for *ea, ei,* &c. If they had not this wider capacity for sound-expression, the object of adding them to the original alphabet would not be intelligible, because the separate characters are there already. So in the case of the group representing *st,* these letters already exist outside it, and it may fairly be said the group would be superfluous if it did not afford some additional facility as by expressing not only *st* but *s* in all its consonantal, as X expresses *e* in its vocalic, combinations, as *st, sc, sg,* &c. The legend runs—

(C)

Left— $\text{NISIGN}_\text{U}^\text{I}\text{MAQE}_\text{ST}^\text{SC}\text{O}$

Right— BI

Nisignu maq estobi.

There does not appear any name *Estob,* but if the *z* group, as it is called, have the force of *sc* or *sg,* then *Maq esgobi, filius episcopi,* has a literary meaning and an historic significance, which in the general dearth of tangible matter must be highly acceptable.

127. We are here near Dungarvan, formerly the place of residence of Mr. William Williams, now deceased. He was an eager inquirer after Ogham remains, and has left copies, made by himself, of several such inscriptions on monuments no longer forthcoming; but I refrain from using or commenting on copies not capable of verification. Mr. Williams was the discoverer of the Oghams in the cave of Drumlohan, and of many other examples, including an inscribed stone WATERFORD. built into the wall of the old church of Kilrush, a mile west of Dungarvan; I have not seen it, but give Mr. Williams's reading, as corrected by Mr. Brash (Og. Mon., 271). The digits are engraved on artificial stem-lines incised on the surface, not, as usual, on the arrises.

Left line— *Forgere,*
Right „ *acmaglumusor,*

which Mr. Brash reads as the monument of Forgereac son of Lumusor. If so, *mag* should be deemed equivalent to *maq* and *maqi.* The sequence *Maglu,* however, may suggest doubts as to the right segregation of *mag.*

128. From Dungarvan, the high road leads to Youghall, *Ardmore* with a detour to Ardmore, intermediate on the sea-coast. 40 *u. c.* Ardmore is a place of high ecclesiastical antiquity, formerly the see of a bishop, retaining what must be regarded as the most complete of the numerous ecclesiastical Round Towers *Round Tower.* in Ireland. In the cathedral churchyard, near the tower, stands an ancient oratory called *Leaba Deglain,* or the Bed of *Saint Declan's* Declan, the reputed first bishop. It is one of the stone *bed.* oratories of the Island MacDara type, made known to architectural antiquaries by Petrie, and reproduces the outlines of some of the sepulchral cellæ of the Burgundian Museum. In its eastern wall there was formerly built in as part of the masonry a stone now preserved within the unroofed walls of the cathedral, Ogham-inscribed on three of its angles. One (A) arris bears a legend singularly like that at old Island—

CAQOMAGECAFEQIO^S_F

Caqomageca feqi of.

• Another—

LUGUDECCASMAQI

Lugudeccas Maqi.

And the third, which bears a seemingly Latin aspect, as I read it—

OE
DOLATIBIGAISGOBI
&c.

Dolati bigoesgobi.

WATERFORD.

129. Another Ogham inscription preserved at Ardmore reads *amadu, insipiens,* and a third, in the collection of the Royal Irish Academy, is a fragment reading—

(B)

ANACIMAQI[

Anaci Maqi

Pedigree of St. Declan.

Lugdec and *Anac* are both names in Declan's pedigree. He was of the southern Desi, originally a Meath tribe. His pedigree is traced to that Felemy Rechtmar, whose mother Queen Bani's tomb lately engaged our notice. Having regard to the number of descents in it, there is some difficulty in putting Declan far enough back to be even a contemporary of St. Patrick, but there exists a great body of tradition to the effect that not only did he precede Patrick in his apostleship, but that on Patrick's approach to the south, he with Kieran and Ibar, two other pre-Patrician bishops, contested the authority of the new comer, and effected a compromise based on the recognition of Declan's ecclesiastical supremacy in his own diocese. Dr. Todd has learnedly shown the incompatibility of these statements with the annalistic chronology; but the Life of Declan, which Colgan regarded as of the eighth century, could hardly have been written if, during the Patrician or Palladian period, there had not been a Christian organisation in Munster, whether represented by Declan or not, sufficiently strong to assert a local independence, which might not unnaturally cause it to be afterwards discountenanced, when the new mission had sufficiently established itself.

Lisgrenan or Grange.
38
c

130. North from Ardmore, on the main road from Dungarvan to Youghall, about five miles from the latter place, at the old cemetery of Grange or Lisgrenan, there has lately been recovered a buried monument, inscribed on two arrises. I have not seen it, and take the text from the Rev. E. Barry's letter to Mr. Atkinson (Brash, 414)—

Left arris—   *ansaloti.*
Right „   *d——— maqi mucoi.*

The *ansaloti* is preceded by an initial mark, ➤, which seems to make the *mucoi* of the right arris necessarily terminal.

CHAPTER V.

131. At Youghall we come on the embouchure of the River
Blackwater, ascending which to Villierstown, a station on the *Kiltera*
left bank, we reach, about a mile south of that point, the 29
Killeen of Kiltera, in the parish of Aglish and townland of *l. c.*
Dromore. One of a group of stones here, seemingly the
remains of a cist or sepulchral cell, bears the inscription read
by Mr. Brash—

Collabot muco l (imperfect).

The reading is supported by another example of the same
name from Laharan, in the County of Kerry.

132. We are here on the opposite side of the Commeragh or *Seskinan*
Monavoullagh mountains, from that by which we entered 13
Waterford county ; and, if we proceed in their direction to *l. r.*
the north-east, enter the parish of Seskinan. The old parish
church, now dismantled, stands in a rough but fertile tract of
country, sloping westward from Monavoullagh. To provide
its window sills and lintels, a neighbouring cemetery
appears to have been ransacked of its headstones. Mr.

Brash has found this site in the remains of a Killeen partly included within the bounds of the present graveyard. As might be expected, several of these sills and lintels are Ogham-inscribed. In very few instances, however, can the whole of the legend be seen. One remarkable name, *Sartigurn*, appears on the lintel of the lower window of the west gable, *Cafic*, *Corb*, and *Cir maqi muc* (*oi*) are legible on others. The church cannot be older than the fifteenth century—a singular evidence of the continuing disposition to regard the Killeen as a lawful quarry.

39

133. Returning westward by Cappoquin at the point where the Blackwater, which up to this part of its course runs from west to east along the base of the Knockmeldown and Galtee Mountains, takes its southern direction to the sea at Youghall, we meet with two new names on a broken Ogham

Salter Bridge
21
l c

pillar preserved in the demesne of Salter Bridge. The legend reads—

Omongadias maqi maci bite,

or *maci biti*. The fracture leaves it doubtful if the first be *O mongadias*, but the probability is that the two digits making the *o* belong to some longer antecedent group. *Mongad*, however, appears to be son of *Macibit*, or son of a son of *Bit* or *Ibit*.

134. Ascending the valley of the Blackwater to Lismore, formerly a great ecclesiastical school of the Patrician establishment, we find many remains of old Hiberno-Roman inscriptions, but, as in other like cases already noted, nothing

70.

Oghamic ; and the same observation will apply to Cloyne, the ecclesiastical capital of the rich tract between Youghall and Cork, south of the Blackwater. Nearly central in this tract,

CORK.

however, and thence reaching westwards, begins an almost continuous succession of Ogham sites and monuments extend-

Glenawillen
65
u c.

ing to Kerry and the Atlantic. At Glenawillen, near Midleton, in the parish of Templenacarriga, in an erased rath-cave were found two stones, now in the Royal Cork Institution, one of which (A) bears the name *Colomagni* "Colman" with some undeciphered additions—

COLOMAGNiFeroMaGi

Feromag, the nearest reduction to which I can bring the CORK. remains of the second name, may be *Feramag*, Fermoy, or *Fermac*, a man's name in Oghamic disguise; but so many letters must be guessed at, that I can only affirm its initial to be F, and its terminal letter to be G followed by vowel notches. And the other, as I believe, is the same, of which the cast (B) shows the name *Scottolini*.

135. North-west from Templenacarriga we enter the large *Knockboy* and for the most part upland parish of Dunbulloge. In that portion which slopes down to the valley of the Lee at *52 l. r.* Bealaghamire, in the townland of Knockboy, once stood a very remarkable assemblage of stone monuments and primitive constructions. A square rath enclosed a cairn, two caves, at one side, four great pillar-stones, two of them inscribed; and at the opposite side two other smaller pillars, one inscribed. A third cave existed outside the square enclosure. On visiting the place in 1868, Mr. Brash "was dismayed to find that the great monument had been almost obliterated by the tenant." One pillar, too massive for easy demolition, remained. It bears inscriptions on two angles. One of these Mr. Brash reads—

Artagni.

At Gormlee, in the northern part of the parish, are two other pillar-stones, Ogham-inscribed, but too much worn by weather and the rubbing of cattle, for transliteration.

136. In the direction of Mallow, the adjoining parish of *Burntfort* Mourne Abbey contributes two examples. The first, found *42 l. c.* in a rath-cave in the townland of Burntfort, was, many years ago, deposited in the Royal Cork Institution. It has since disappeared, appropriated, it is supposed, by the masons employed in building the Cork Athenæum (Brash, Og. Mon., 118, n.), but was, about 1849, the subject of much discussion in which all parties were agreed respecting the characters—

Sagittari.

Sagittarius is a known Latinization of proper names signifying bowman or archer. *Fearbogha*, the Irish name, having the same meaning, will probably be regarded as concealed under this classical disguise.

CORK.
Greenhill
42
u. c.

137. The other monument stands at Greenhill. It is a fine pillar, 8 ft. high. The initial characters have been found difficult to decipher (Brash, Og. Mon., 137). By the aid of a cast of this part of the inscription kindly made for me by the Rev. Thomas Olden, Ballyclough, I am satisfied that the initial characters are 'Tr, and see no reason to doubt that the entire legend reads—

Trenu or *Treni maqi mucoi qritti.*

Bweeng
41
l. c.

138. Kilshannig parish, also lying north of Donoughmore, supplies one example. It is apparently a low gravestone close to the Roman Catholic church of Bweeng. It is noticeable for its vowels, formed by stem-crossing digits, and for its Latin termination. Mr. Brash reads it (Og. Mon., 144)—

Mongus.

The *n* and *g* are distinct characters, whence it might be inferred that examples in the more compendious form ⫻ are of more recent times.

138a. At the Royal Cork Institution there is a considerable collection of Ogham-inscribed stones, the description of all save one of which will be found in connection with their places of origin. The one of uncertain origin, but no doubt nearly local, is much abraded and very rough and difficult of decipherment. I make out—

SCOTTALₗaNₗSCOTToL ✱ ✱ ✱

Monataggart
61
u. l.

139. South from Kilshannig, lies the large upland parish of Donoughmore. It occupies the watershed dividing the valleys of the Blackwater and the Lee, its tributary to the former being the Clyda running northward to Mallow, and to the latter, the Dripsey running southward to Coachford. The Dripsey, near Brew Bridge, runs below the slopes of a high-lying farm called Monataggart. On this farm, several years ago, the occupier, in ploughing, found some great stones under the surface, forming a kind of chamber, or rather pit, which contained black earth and ashes interspersed with broken pottery. The stones on being removed were found to bear long and unusually perfect Ogham inscriptions. At first the presence of the ashes and pottery suggested the

idea of sepulchral cremation; but these objects might also CORK.
indicate a boundary mark. The Roman Agrimensores were
not the only functionaries who marked boundaries of land by
the deposit of ashes and potsherds. Martin, in his memoir of
the Western Islands, has noticed the practice in several
places where Roman customs could hardly be supposed to
have penetrated. The object was, no doubt, to leave something indestructible as a memorial, and the practice is probably
old European rather than Roman. Here, then, if anywhere,
we might look for evidences confirmatory of the allusions to
the use of Ogham in the Brehon Laws. The Bishop of
Limerick has lately collected them. " How many ever- *Allusions to*
burning candles are there by which perpetual ownership of *Ogham in the Brehon Laws,*
land is secured? Memorials of the Historians, of Ancient *collected by*
Writings, in Ancient Mounds." " The joint Memorial of two *the Bishop of Limerick.*
Territories, *i.e.*, The Ogam in the Gallan (pillar-stone), or it
might be the evidence of two neighbours." Again, " To
decide by the recital of a rock, *i.e.*, that the name of the man
who bought [the land] be in the bond of Ogam, *i.e.*, that the
Ogam of the purchase be in the flag of a mound." Nothing,
indeed, indicating purchase or territorial designation has as
yet been found on any of the buried Ogham-inscribed stones
hitherto offered to notice; but if the ashes deposited in
this pit really indicate a boundary mark, one could hardly
look on the names recorded on the stones contained in it as
other than those of proprietors taking this method of per-
petuating the evidence of their titles. The forms of the
inscriptions, however, do not encourage this idea. Three of
them are now in the collection of the Royal Irish Academy.
One of these (A) is in the simplest "A son of B " form—

Dalagni maqi dali. (A)

140. The other two have more of the religious aspect. The
Camp inscription affords the key to one. It must be read from 72.
left to right inversely, giving each character the value of its
opposite in the Ogham scale—

Feqreq moqoi glunlegget. (B)

that is, the stone of " Fiachra, son (or of the sons) of Glunlegget." Observe the departure from the hitherto constant

form of *Maqi*, and note the approach to something like pre-dication in the apparent meaning of *Glunlegget*, " the Kneeler." Possibly also I might not misinterpret what may be in some of my readers' minds, if I queried whether this means the Son of the Kneeler, or the Kneeler or Penitent of the Son. It will doubtless have been observed that, up to the present, there has been no direct mention in any of these legends, however Christian and religious in their general aspect, of the name of our Lord; and that *Maqi*, in some of its numerous contexts, can hardly be referred on any intelligible principles to the person commemorated.

(C)

141. The third monument from Monataggart now in the Academy is in the " qui fuit " form, and savours of the ascetic fashion of self-humiliation. It reads in the usual way—

44

Broenienas poi netattrenalugos.

It also seems to predicate of Broenienas that he was " neta," if that be a separate vocable, and whatever meaning it may have, of some one called Trenloc—champion of Tenloc, for instance,—or, if " neta " be part of a longer name, that Broenienas (before taking that name in religion) had been secularly, Netatrenloc. These two latter monuments are fine pillar-stones of about 8 ft. in length, and obviously intended to be set up on end.

142. A fourth inscribed pillar remains at Monataggart built into the fence of the road leading into the farmyard. It is not inscribed on the arris, neither has it any actual stem-line, but depends for its interpretation on the adjustment of its digits to an imaginary line. It is the most delicately-incised of all

103.

the examples so far observed. Some of the digits are even shorter than the minuscules of Killeen-Cormac, and all are cut with extreme fineness.

(C)

$$\text{FERGOSOMACI}^{LL'}_{S}\text{OM}^{I}_{UU}\text{NACCA.}$$

The dimensions of the pit are stated to have been about 5 ft. long, 3½ ft. broad, and 3 ft. deep. It is now filled up, and the site restored to agriculture. Whence the stones came from, or why deposited there, are questions hard to answer. There is a disused burial-ground on the opposite

bank of the Dripsey a little higher up, at Kilcullen, where *Cork.*
one pillar-stone, stated to bear the legend *Lugu decces maqi* *Kilcullen*
ott, is still standing. I saw it in an unfavourable light, which *61 u r.*
may account for my being unable either to verify or correct
the reading; but the spot is evidently one of the *Killeen* class
so often noticed and to be noticed. To drag the Monataggart
pillars across the deep valley and bed of the river, would have
been a very difficult operation. The most reasonable solution
would, perhaps, be that the place—as its name, "Priests'
Marsh," imports—had possessed some kind of Christian cell
before its conversion to farming purposes, and that the stones
of its cemetery had been utilised for the construction of this
Kist-vaen, which need not necessarily be supposed to have
been either agrimensorial or sepulchral in its character, or of
any great antiquity.

143. Westward of Kilcullen, the country becomes more
bare and lonely, until, at a place called Barrachauran, we *Barrachauran*
find ourselves in presence of very imposing megalithic mixed *49, 50 l. r.*
with smaller stone remains. Many great stones have been
broken up, some lie prostrate, and some are still standing.
One group of these, three in number, makes a very imposing *Imposing*
and even solemn feature in the wide green upland. The *megalithic monument.*
highest, which I judge to be about 14 ft. above the ground,
bears the remains of a much-effaced Ogham on one of its
angles, now almost obliterated by the rubbing of cattle. It
is undoubtedly an Ogham of the regular digit and notch
kind, but of what purport it is impossible now to say. If
sepulchral, one would hesitate to suppose it Christian. If a
territorial landmark, it might be expected to stand alone.
The impression produced by the view of the place is that it
has been a cemetery in which, whether Pagan or Christian in
its origin, the megalith has been associated with the humbler
grave-stone. A neighbouring rath-cave has supplied one of
these smaller memorials, now in the Royal Cork Institution—

CARRTTACCGAQIM^U_OcCAGMa.

Carrtaccgaqi Muc [*agma*?]

10.

—an example of the difficulty of distinguishing the *g* from
m m. But I take it to be as first given, and equivalent to the
British *caractac*.

144. To the west of Donoughmore we enter the parish of Aghabulloge. It is still the same upland country, sloping upward to the north towards the watershed between the valleys of the Blackwater and Lee, and to the west towards the Boggra Mountains. About the middle of the parish is the church of St. Olan. In the churchyard, set up among modern graves, stands what is regarded as St. Olan's pillar-stone, although the legend which it bears does not commemorate him by that name. It is an object of great veneration, and ever since it was first noticed has been crowned with a separate cap-stone. The old cap-stone has disappeared, and a modern one has been recently substituted. The belief regarding it is, that to whatever distance it may be removed it will be found next day in its old place. The same belief exists respecting several other supposed sacred stones in Ireland. It is a very widespread superstition, and not without example among the Greeks. The pillar is inscribed nearly from end to end, and has to be raised to get at the beginning of the legend. This comprises two of the ✗ formed characters, and begins with the letters *anm* already noticed as an initial formula. No real difficulty exists in any of the following characters, save in one group of two digits which, with certain vowel notches, precede the second ✗. The group as it presents itself on the worn surface would read *bm*, which might be the result of the upper half of one digit of an original *g* having disappeared through abrasion or other accident. In the *b* combination it will not assimilate with what goes either before or after in any vocalisable combination. But if we be content to assume that the group is a *g* of which the upper half of the first digit has been lost, and to suppose the space following to be occupied with vowel notches equivalent to its length, making a probable *u*, then the reading becomes intelligible and relevant—

P　　　　　　e *G* a P

ANMCORREAMAQFUIDDaI*BM*uEATT

&c.　　　　　　&c.

Anm Corpimaq fuidd (e)g(u)ptt.

The digits forming the terminal *t* have a cross-bar, intimating a contraction. We have had a suspicion of the employment of

Latin in *feci* at Drumloghan. We are already familiar with
poi as the equivalent of *qui fuit*. *Fuit*, in old Irish spelling
would be *fuid*, as, under *delg*, " a pin," in Cormac's Glossary
" deleg, ex quo legid (a ligat) duas partes togæ." The
inscription then would be read as if *qui fuit* followed the name
Cormac, here shown in its inflated form of Corpimaq, "who
was"—whatever the last word of the legend predicates of
him. The last word seems to complete the sentence not
doubtfully, " Who was the Egyptian." But why expect to
find Egyptians in Ireland? The answer must again be
drawn from the Litany of Ængus, where, amongst other visi-
tants, he enumerates " the seven Egyptian monks who lie in
Disert Ulad." I do not suppose that St. Olan's is Disert Ulad;
but, amid such a concourse of foreigners, it will not surprise
us if we find an ecclesiastic of the Egyptian rule, even here
in Aghabulloge in Cork, as we already had some ground for
recognising the record of an Italian one among the rounded
cope-stones of Ballintaggart in Kerry. But that an Egyptian,
or a monk of the Egyptian rule should be called Cormac, will,
no doubt, appear strange. There were, however, so many
names of origin, of endearment, of personal traits, of personal
incidents, as well as names in religion in use among these
early Irish monks and clerics, that Corpimaq as a *nomen*
adoptivum need cause no sense of incongruity. Olan, however, is the name which has traditionally clung to the patron
of Aghabulloge, whether in connection with his pillar-stone,
his church, or his holy well. And so far everything points to
the *Corpmac* of the inscription as an *alias* of this holy person.
Could we distinctly identify him, we might have a reasonable assurance of standing on firmer ground than any we
have yet felt under us. And this identification has, I think,
really been demonstrated. The Book of Leinster records
Eolang as venerated at Aghabulloge. Under the name of
Evolengus the Bishop of Limerick finds him commemorated
as "institutor," which may mean " tutor " or " initiator," of St.
Finbarr, of Cork; and further, that he had the *alias* name
of *MacCorbius*. In the Irish life of St. Finbarr his baptiser
is a bishop called *MacCuirb*. Finbarr died A.D. 621. Taken
altogether, the identification seems complete, and puts the

CORK.

monument of *Corpmac* back to some time in the latter part of the sixth century. If, then, prior to A.D. 600, Ogham writing had passed into its secondary stage, time for an antecedent course of development should be found, for which the intermediate period from Palladius might hardly seem sufficient.

St. Olan's well
61
l. l.

145. Olan's or Evolengus's holy well, stands eastward at a little distance from the cemetery. It is stone-domed, and overshadowed by a venerable tree. A great slab, which formerly served as a foot bridge over a stream at the opposite side of the church, has been set up beside the well. It bears the rudely-cut Ogham inscription—

97.

No maqi dego.

The tree, the stone vault, the trickling stream, and the standing stone make an agreeable feature in the bare surrounding country.

146. The neighbourhood has formerly been full of raths, rath-caves, and those deserted burying grounds, of which so much has already been said. Of the numerous inscriptions supplied by this lettered moorland, one is from a *Killeen* in the townland of Knockrour, now in the possession of Colonel Lane Fox. It has been read—

Knockrour
60
l. l.

$$\text{MUDDOSSAM(A)QQ}^{\text{AA}}_{\text{O}}\text{T};$$

Muddossa maqqa at;

but the singularity of the names suggests, as preferable, the reverse inverted reading, also countenanced by the fact that the stone is fractured at the terminal digits.

$$]\ \text{s}^{\text{f a}}_{\text{n o}}\text{onn mac collum.}$$

147. From the neighbouring lands of Deelish, in a similar burying-place called Liads, another example has been transferred to the Royal Cork Institution, inscribed on two angles—

Liads
60
l. c.

Left arris   OTMAQIMAQIRITE.
                ot maqi maqi rite.

Right „   ]COICORIBIRI.
                coi coribiri.

The reading is not continuous. Each arris is read upward. CORK.
Coi may be portion of *mucoi*, or it may have a separate meaning. *Coribiri* is another example of the use of the union
vowel in inflating such proper names as *Corbri*.

148. In the northern part of the parish where it slopes up
to the Machera mountain, in the townland of Glounaglogh, *Glounaglogh*
formerly stood a circle of pillar-stones. One of these is 60
inscribed. It is now in the Royal Cork Institution. The *u. c.*
inscription is broken off at top.

U
GUNAGVSSOSEMA[
I

The name, here and elsewhere, seems an inflated form of
Congus, Cungus. Whether the *uma* is a separate vocable or
part of some other combination, cannot be determined. The
ma, perhaps, is part of a lost *maqi*, in which case it might be
thought that *u* is a qualifying particle, used as *ot* and *o* in
other instances.

There are many remaining examples from this fruitful field,
but they are fragmentary and uncertain.

149. Between Aghabulloge and the Lee intervenes the
parish of Magourney. A rude pillar inscribed on two natural
ridges of one face from Tulligmore in this parish is also at the *Tulligmore*
Cork Institution. Mr. Brash (Og. Mon., 29) reads it— 61
l c.

Maqi Laseg.
Ot Maqi He.

Whether *ot* be a proper name or a qualifying adjunct of *Maqi*,
may be questionable. I have not a cast of this legend, and
speak with reserve. I could not determine the first name,
and for *He* my drawing, possibly erroneous, has *De*.

150. Let us now pass from the table-land dividing the
waters of the Blackwater and Lee, and crossing the Lee
southward, enter on the corresponding upland forming the
watershed between the Lee and the Bandon. In this extensive tract are four rath-caves, in the construction of
which Ogham-inscribed monuments have been employed.
Killeens and Cealuraghs adjoin them all, and, no doubt,
have supplied the stones. The first is situate in the *Ballyhank*
parish of Kilnaglory, six miles east from Cork City. Its 85.

CORK.

various chambers extend through a length of 52 ft., and it has yielded six Ogham examples. One of them was presented to the Royal Irish Academy; the remaining five were acquired by the late Mr. Windele; but, since his death, the entire collection has been reunited in the Academy's Lapidary Museum. Two other monuments of the same class, of uncertain history, were among the Windele collection, and have also been acquired by the Academy. All, save the first, are extremely rude. None of them bears any symbol of Christianity, though the legends are characteristic of ascetic fashion, *olc* and *corb*, " bad," " wicked," entering into four of the names. The Ballyhank group read respectively—

SACATTINI
ULCCAGNI
CoRBAGNI
[CO]CORotaNI
GG
CoRBA　N
ST　Q　i
&c.

46.

41.

In this last, stem-crossing digits are exceptionally used for vowels.

151. The sixth example yields the more predicative legend—

Maqi elliaci o Maqi Ni,

97.

with another line, now illegible, running up the face of the pillar, which is of extraordinary coarseness and ruggedness. I am unable to say what the *o* before *maqi* may mean. The characters are capable of being read *o maniqi*, being partly on the head and partly carved down the arris of the stone.

152. The other of uncertain origin cannot be said to bear any inscription, but is covered with lines and digits sculptured possibly in imitation of Oghams or Runes, or, it may be, in a *quasi* Ogham still unexplained. There is a great abundance of such *pseudo* Oghams in the south of Ireland, but it would not be possible here to notice them in detail.

Rev. D. Haigh. His History of the Forrtigurn stone.

153. The Ballyhank monument, however, of most interest, is the one mentioned to have been first acquired by the Academy. It is a small, smooth slab, which has been engraved with care and delicacy, and preserves a remarkable name, Forrtigurn. It had quite a fascination for the mind of the late Rev. Daniel Haigh, who conceived this to be the

name of the British king Vortigern, the inviter of the Saxons. Cork.
Vortigern was an ally of the Irish Scots. After the loss of
his kingdom and the denunciations of Saint German, he disappeared—some say burnt by fire from heaven; others,
swallowed up by the earth; others, in exile. His son Pascent
continued the struggle, and resorted for aid to Ireland,
whence he returned with the Irish *Gillamorus* as his ally.
Ireland was, at that time, the ordinary place of refuge for
dethroned British princes and unsuccessful British insur-
gents. Pascent was also accompanied by *Eopa* or *Eobba*,
who served him by carrying off his competitor by poison.
Digits which, among other readings, might yield the
name *hioba*, are carved in very small minuscular Ogham
on the opposite arris of the stone. It is a remarkable name, *Vortigern,*
unique, I believe, in Ogham records, and, if Mr. Haigh's *King of*
Britain, father
reading be the true one, gives a good countenance to his belief *of Saint*
that it was this *Eobba* who caused the monument to be en- *Faustus.*
graved. But to whose memory engraved, is the difficulty.
Vortigern had a daughter, the mother, by his own incest, of
Saint Faustus; and they perished or disappeared together.
The word which introduces the patronymic is not *maqi*, but
moqi, which Mr. Haigh takes to mean "daughter." The
name of Vortigern's daughter has never been divulged in
history, so that its non-appearance here need not excite
surprise. But there is the appearance of some suppression or
obscuration of some name going before *moqi*. There are five
underline digits preceded by the vowel *a*. Normally they
would read *n*, but the central one is distinguished from the
pairs flanking it by being very delicately, while they are
strongly, cut. Reading up to this digit we would have *alb*,
and, resiling thence and commencing anew as if all were
normal, we would complete *Alban*, which at one time I
thought might be the meaning. But I now rather imagine
the slender line to be what in Runic writing is called an
"elegance" or caprice of the engraver, and that the legend
should be read—

ANMOQIFORaRTIGURN.

an moqi Forrtigurn.

An map, in Welsh, intimates bastardy, or something worse,

H

and the use of its equivalent here is quite consistent with Mr. Haigh's theory. Vortigern's epoch has generally been fixed in relation to that of St. Germanus of Auxerre, which would put the closing events of his reign in the post-Palladian period. But there is a difficulty in bringing him down to so late a date. He had been son-in-law of Maximus, who died A.D. 389, and the wild, mystical, and romantic incidents of his story are better suited to a struggle with some British ecclesiastic than with the great bishop of Auxerre, whose biographer and immediate successor, Constans, does

*His son
Pascent.*

not so much as mention Vortigern's name. If his son Pascent procured the aid of an Irish king whose name sounds in Christianity, he could hardly have been sought for in the eastern or northern parts of the island: but if there were then a Christian community in Munster, the British narrative in this respect would be consistent. In any case, the Ballyhank " Fortigern " stone will probably be considered one of the most interesting and possibly most precious monuments of the early existence of an Irish and British connection.

*Roovesmore
72
l. l.*

154. Eight miles further we stwardwe reach Rooer's Bridge on the Lee, adjoining which, in the townland of Roovesmore, parish of Eglish, there existed some years ago a cave in the remains of a rath, which the farmer, desiring to utilise the land, has since erased. The cave contained three Ogham-inscribed stones of the same general character as those at Ballyhank and Drumloghan. They are now deposited in the British Museum, and have been described with remarkable accuracy, both in the particulars of their deposit and of the legends inscribed on them, by Colonel Lane Fox. They are all engraved on both arrises.

One reads—

> *Maqi falamni.*
> *Maqi Ercias.*

The one name being new in its formation *mn*, where hitherto we have been accustomed to *gn*; the other an echo, in name and formation, of the Dunmore Head example.

155. The second legend is marked by several peculiarities. Digits crossing the line are employed for vowels; in some places large and wide apart, in others very small and closely Cork. spaced. Colonel Lane Fox's drawing reads—

tabira mocoi sug——— fedacu.

The latter name, if read inversely to the opposite characters, would be *usale*—a known name in archaic pedigrees, where it is written *usalec* (Pedigree of Brendan). I know of no name in old Irish literature beginning with *Sug*, save one *Siugmall* which occurs in the Archaic pedigrees of the Book of Invasions. The initial *Ta* of the first name is not on my cast, which possibly arises from oversight in not placing it low enough on the stone; and the only points on which I express a doubt are, whether the name has a terminal *a*, and whether an *a* do not precede the imperfect terminal *Sog*, or whatever letter the terminal digits may be part of. In any case the feminine-looking *bira* tends to confirm Mr. Haigh's theory of the meaning of *mocoi*.

156. The third Roovesmore stone is a shapely pillar 7 ft. high, with what would be a continuous inscription but for a fracture at top, in which, however, I believe one vowel point only has been lost—

anaflamattias muco (i) eluri afi a (χ) eras ;   39

or, if the reader shift his position on coming to the second arris—

anaflamattias muco (i) eduriati a (χ) erac.   8.

The flanking vowels make it impossible that (χ) here should have the power of *ea*, and neither *aperas* nor *aperac* seems to offer anything normal. The Bishop of Limerick has lately suggested for χ the third power of *dh*, which no one acquainted with the varying forces given to Runic letters will consider unprecedented. If extended to *th*, it might help us to more likely-looking results both in this and other examples which remain to be noticed.

157. Southward from Roovesmore, in the parish of Temple-martin, six miles northward from Bandon, at Garranes, Mr. *Garranes* Brash notices the remarkable legend— 84 *l c.*

C(a)ssitt(a)s maqi mucoi Calliti.

The stone bearing it appears to have come from a rath-cave, and in the near neighbourhood is a *Killeen* (Og. Mon., 158).

158. At about an equal distance south-west from Bandon, at Aghaliskey, in the parish of Kilmaloda, another rath-cave, originally explored by Mr. Windele, is described by Mr. Brash. He reads on the fourth roofing lintel from the entrance the legend—

Girognq,

where analogy would lead us to expect *i* instead of *q*: but Mr. Brash states his impression that the inscription was originally longer (Og. Mon., 146).

159. On the seventh lintel from the entrance, on two raised ridges of the under face, he reads—

Qunagusos Maqi mucoi F——,

remarking that the stone has been built in without regard to the course of reading, which, as the stone lies, seems to be from right to left (*ib.* 146).

160. These legends on the roofing stones were known to the original explorers. Mr. Brash discovered another on a supporting pillar.

" The upright pillar is 4 ft. 3 in. in length, and 12 in. by 6 in. at the centre, and of somewhat lesser dimensions at the top and bottom. To my extreme delight I found it to bear a perfect inscription cut with the greatest accuracy and care, and looking as fresh as if engraved yesterday The letter-scores are the smallest I have yet seen, being short, and finely but deeply cut. They appear not to have been punched, but formed by rubbing with a sharp tool and water. . . . . . Its (the stone's) position in the cave, with the inscribed angle turned to the wall, preserved it from injury through the long round of centuries it must have lain here concealed. The inscription is as follows :—

Coi bagni maqi mucoi.

It commences 2 ft. 3 in. from the bottom, and occupies but 1 ft. 9 in. of the angle."—(Og. Mon., 147.)

From these statements we should regard the *coi* as a distinct vocable and not as the termination of a mutilated *mucoi*; unless, indeed, the five digits of the *i* be stem-crossing = *r*, which would give the familiar *Corbagni*. As regards the fully-expressed *mucoi*, if this be the only inscription on the CORK. pillar, it must certainly be taken as an instance of *mucoi* terminal, with such inferences respecting its grammatical relation to *Maqi* as may follow from that consideration.

161. Another rath-cave, which had long been closed, at Cooldorrihy, in the parish of Kilmichael, about midway *Cooldorrihy* between Bandon and Macroom, was reopened, in 1870, for 82 Mr. Brash. He found the supporting pillar of one of the *c.* roofing lintels inscribed with a legend, which he reads—

Feqoanai maqi Eaqod.

The *Ea* is represented by X; the terminal character questionable (Og. Mon., 160).

162. In the same parish, on the lands of Knockouran, or *Mount Music* Mount Music, formerly stood the pillar selected by Mr. 82 Windele for his own monument, and now, I believe, erected *u. r.* in the garden of his former residence at Blairs Hill, Cork. It *Ogham-* bears a deeply-incised Maltese cross with the legend— *inscribed pillar stone, selected by Mr. Windele for his own monument.*

$$\text{ANNACCA}_{\text{NN}}^{\text{SS}}\text{IMA}_{\text{R}}^{\text{Q}}\text{IAILLITT}_{\text{N}}^{\text{R}}.$$

The alternative readings are caused, first, by a doubt whether the groups following *annaca* are of four or five digits each; next, by faint but visible protractions downward of the five outline digits forming *prima facie* the Q of *Maqi*; and, lastly, by the ambiguous relation of the final group to the line of arris, some of its digits distinctly, and others not at all appearing to cross the angle; but to my eye forming R rather than N. If the legend be taken as in the ordinary formula of "A son of B," it would read, disregarding the protractions—

$$\text{Annaca}_{nn}^{ss}i \ maqi \ Aillitt(a)n.$$

The last vocable being a proper name. But if it be, as I suppose it is, *Aillittr*, a "pilgrim," there arises a strong presumption that a double reading of *maqi* is intended—

Annacassi mayi Mari aillittr.

163. About twelve miles westward from Macroom, in the *Shanacloon* parish of Ballyvourney, at Shanacloon, is a pillar bearing a 58 *l. c.*

CORK.

legend, read by Mr. Brash, omitting initial characters imperfect.

* * *Bir Maqi.*

(Og. Mon., 153.)

Coomliah
106
u. r.

164. In the mountainous country between Ballyvourney and Bantry, at Coomliah East, in the parish of Kilmocamogue, stands an inscribed pillar now mutilated. Its legend was transcribed by Mr. Windele while it was still entire. It appears by this copy (Og. Mon.) to have terminated with the syllable *grac.* The preceding characters are not legible.

165. South of Bantry, that portion of the peninsula separating Bantry Bay from the estuary of Kenmare, contains two examples. The first stands near Inchintaglin Bridge on the north side of the Adrigoole river, beside the old church of

Kilcaskan
103
l. r.

Kilcaskan. Mr. Brash reads the principal name *Luguqrit,* and makes the whole legend, which is much defaced,

Luguqrit maqi qritti.

Ballycrovane
102
u. c.

166. The other example is found on the western shore of the peninsula, on the margin of the Kenmare river at Ballycrovane, in the parish of Kilcashmore. We have passed in review many great Ogham-inscribed pillar-stones, but this is by much the grandest example of such a monument in

Obelisk 25 ft.
in length.

Ireland. It is really a fine obelisk, 25 ft. in total length, and of graceful proportions, although, like all monuments of its class, untouched by the stonecutter. I have not seen it, but take its dimensions from Mr. Brash, and what I say of its site and appearance, from a characteristic drawing by Mr. Windele. Its inscription, from the agreement of almost all the transcripts, is, I have no doubt, as given by Mr. Brash in the sequence—

Maqideceddasafitoranias.

If read *decedda,* the name of the person commemorated would be Safitoran (like *Saffigeg*); if read *deceddas,* it would be *afi =* grandson of Toran. In either case, Decedda should be taken as a proper name; and it seems a likely Oghamic form of Deagad, from whom a widespread family of the Hy-Deagaid, inhabiting this region, descended. We have had many examples of it in conjunction with *Maqi* in widely-separated districts of KERRY. Ireland, and two others elsewhere have still to be mentioned— both in Roman characters, though the monuments are Celtic, —one in Anglesea, *hic jacet Maccudeceti* ; and one in Devon, *Sarini filii Maccodecheti.* I think we may be quite assured that the Clan Deagaid had its original seats in Munster, and that if it spread to Anglesea and Devon, and commemorated itself monumentally there as well as in Kildare and Kerry, the Irish claim to a colony in Britain capable of found- ing a school of Ogham writing would be very cogently evidenced. But it seems highly improbable that an individual proper name should be so widely diffused; and we cannot forget that in the first example we had of the same formula, it was accompanied by the Christian cross. These considera- tions raise a question not to be lightly dismissed : Whether, in this as in other cases, *maqi* means "son" in ordinary pedigree, or "the" Son in theology, the formula in the latter view designating some office or relation to our Lord ? If that were so, the megalithic character of other monuments would present no objection to their having been raised in Christian times.

167. Ascending the estuary to Kenmare, there is found at a place called Cappagh, in the townland of Dromatouk, a *Dromatouk* *Killeen* or disused burial-place marked by several standing 93 stones, one of which is inscribed. Mr. Brash reads it— *u. c.*

anm otunilocid maqi Alott.

The *anm* is easily separable, as are the *maqi* and *alott*, the last being an archaic name of frequent occurrence in this region. As to *otunilocid*, whether it be one proper name or divisible, Mr. Brash expresses no opinion (Og. Mon., 221).

168. Eastward from Kenmare, in the parish of Kilgarvan, *Lomanagh* at Lomanagh, the name *Ottin*, apparently the first member of 94 the vocables last mentioned, is read by Mr. Brash on a fine *c* pillar-stone in this connection—

Ottinn maqi Fecm.

169. Half a mile south from Lomanagh, in a *Killeen* sur- rounded by a stone circle, at Gortmacaree, formerly stood a *Gortmacaree* pillar, now at Adare Manor, which Mr. Brash reads— 84 *l. c.*

Noar or Nur maqi Farudran.

Derrygurrane
92
u. l.

170. Retracing the line of the Kenmare estuary, on the northern side, in Templenoe parish, an inscribed pillar is found within a stone circle at Derrygurrane South. Mr. Brash transliterates it—

Anm Crunan maqi Luqisma.

(Og. Mon., 194.)

The Bishop of Limerick makes it—

Anm Crunan macu lucuin.

(Proc. R. I. A., 1 s. s., 157.)

If the former be correct, it might, in its terminal syllable, offer some analogy to the first legend at Rath Croghan.

Dromkeare
98
u c.

171. Proceeding westward, at Dromkeare, in Dromod parish, near Loch Currane, a much-abraded inscription is read doubtfully—

Tudenn maqi menlenn.

(Og. Mon., 215.)

Killogrone
80
l. l.

172. At Killogrone, parish of Caher, in a *Killeen*, formerly stood a cross-signed, inscribed pillar, now transferred to the grounds of the Convent of Christian Brothers at Cahirciveen. The legend exhibits several examples of the employment of those *sigla* from the *Forfeada* which stand respectively for *o* and *e* in their diphthongal combinations. It has been examined and read by the Bishop of Limerick—

Anm Moeleagoemir admaci Feacimean.

(Proc. R. I. A., 1 s. s., 157.)

Bishop Graves refers to many examples to justify his acceptance of *anm* as an abbreviated equivalent of *anima*, or, it may be, of *oratio pro anima*, giving to the legend the meaning of (a prayer for the soul of) *Maeladhamar* misborn son of *Feacimean* (or *Feacim*) ; and observes that the *admaci* allies itself with the *otmaqi* of one of the monuments in the Royal Cork Institution already mentioned ; intimating, at the same time, his opinion that it implies something to the discredit of the deceased, for which reason, he suggests, the inscription has been carved on the end of the stone remote from the cross, and so presumably intended to be hidden in

the ground. He also remarks that the pillar stood, at Killo- Residue of Kerry.
grone, at the heading of a grave, and that a lower stone
marked the foot with an elaborate cross and a dove engraved
upon it in a very peculiar manner. *Moeleagoemir* appears to
be characteristically Christian, and *Feacimean* to be a more
dignified presentation of the patronymic found at Lomanagh.

173. Bishop Graves also appears to have examined the
inscribed stone at Killeenadreena, in the Island of Valentia, *Killeenadreena*
which Mr. Brash reads as on his authority—

Logoqi maqi erenan.

174. In the direction ·of the Lakes of Killarney, on a site
among the mountains near Lough Carra, another inscribed
stone has lately been discovered. The Bishop of Limerick
describes it as expressing the single name—

galeotas.

175. Further east, in the direction of Killorglin, the Finglass
River, descending from the Reeks, runs under the slope of
a green eminence in the townland of Kilcolaght East, the site *Kilcolaght*
of another Killeen, now marked by one standing pillar and   65
several prostrate fragments of others, all Ogham-inscribed.   *u. t.*
The standing pillar is inscribed on all its four angles. On
one face (south) it presents the legend—

QRIGIFIQQ
Qrigifiqq,   (A)

or, read reversely, *nnitigern*; but I take it to be a variety of
the Cattufiq and Kellufic type. On the opposite angle what
remains exhibits some appearance of that kind of double
reading noticed in connection with the Mount Music example. ·
There seem to be remains of

Sigangng$^e_1$lmari,

but the digits of the *n* are protracted in fainter lines on the
upper edge, as if possibly intended also to yield the name *Mari*.
This, however, may be the effect of weathering, not design.
On the north face it shows a legend beginning *anm fir* . . . .,
but the remainder is to me illegible.

Another fragment shows—

$$]OCCMAQILO\tilde{N}GRI\overset{i}{}\overset{R}{}\begin{smallmatrix}T\\F\end{smallmatrix}[$$

(B)

occ maqi logri(n),

recalling the British Locrin.

Another—

(C)

urg,

which may have been a Pictish Urgust, or its cognate Furgas.

Another—

(D)

$$]GGOMAQIGIL\begin{smallmatrix}L\\S\end{smallmatrix}[$$

aggo maqi agill,

or, perhaps, *gill,* suggestive of a Christian designation in *gilla.*

And a fifth, more complete, yields an additional example of these strange names in *fic,* already observed on—

(E)

$$RITTUFFECCMAQiMaF\begin{smallmatrix}I\\UU\end{smallmatrix}DDON\begin{smallmatrix}A\\O\end{smallmatrix}S$$

Rittuffecc maqi f—ddonas.

All marks of a surrounding enclosure have disappeared, but the site is still respected. The scene is touching and impressive; and one asks again and again, Why should the remains of these Qrigifics and Rittufics be deemed unworthy to mingle with baptised clay?

176. Proceeding in the direction of Whitefield, the seat of The Macgillicuddy, one reaches, at a ford and stepping-stones on the Glasheen Cockmuck stream, descending from the Reeks, the poor hamlet and ruined church of Kilgobinet. In the "street" of the eastern part of the village is a roundish stone lying flat, bearing in Ogham the inscription—

ANNAFEN.

In an adjoining meadow to the north is another with a longer legend, which, owing to an accident to the cast, I cannot answer for. I failed to find here the pillar stone alleged on the authority of a sketch by Mr. Windele to bear the seemingly abnormal name, *Dugunnggunns.* A Killeen adjoins the village.

177. At Whitefield there was formerly assembled a collection of Ogham monuments from the adjoining district.
Two of these are now in the Museum of the Royal Irish
Academy. The first inscribed on two angles, not continuously—

Nocati maqi maqi rette.

"Nocat, son of the son of Rett"; and

Maqi mucoi uddami,

nearly the last of the many examples of this obscure formula.

The second Whitefield example furnishes something more
tangible—

Alatto celi battigni.

It was customary, and after the sixth century, for pious
persons to designate themselves as *celi*, or devotees of certain
saints, and of God, as the *celide*. Alatto,—the genitive apparently of the archaic name Alott,—is here the *celi* of Battignus.
There are many Boithins, saints in the Irish Calendar. We
have then here an Ogham record presumably of a late date,
and eminently Christian, though without cross or other symbol.

178. Between the Reeks and the Laune, near where the
river is crossed by Beaufort Bridge, is the well-known
Cave of Dunloe. It is roofed with Ogham-inscribed slabs,
and internally propped by an Ogham-inscribed pillar. The
pillar bears on one angle the name of Ptolemaic note in the
district, *Cunacena.* Of the inscribed roofing stones the outer
one only, owing to the ends of the others being inserted in the
masonry of the walls, is fully legible. It exhibits the X
character in a context which rejects the *ea* value, and, with
the *p* value, yields a vocable so odd as a proper name,
toicap, that one is disposed to look with favour on the suggestion of a third value *dh*, which I would venture to extend
to *th*, and so read—

dego maqi mocoi toicathi.

Inside, we find the names of Rittiq, Tal, Forgos, but in
incomplete contexts. The cave, I believe, was stripped many
years ago by the Bishop of Limerick, from whom I trust,
while he is still spared to the world of learning, we may some
day expect full readings.

179. Crossing Beaufort Bridge, and proceeding a short distance in the direction of Milltown, we come on the ruined church of Kilbonane, giving name to the parish which embraces both banks of the Laune, and, along the river on both banks, presents much sylvan and pastoral beauty. The

Ruined Church of Kilbonane. church is in the open country behind. It seems a thirteenth or fourteenth century building. At the north side of the altar is a grave covered in with a long flag of red sandstone, broken across the middle. The arrises and flat of the slab are occupied with lines of Ogham, there being three lines on the flat, independent of those on the two arrises. Looking where the commencement of the inscription should be, the surface is uninscribed. Further on it seems to begin *Agni Maqi*, followed by a string of names in the Latin genitive form. Seeking for the earlier portion of the principal name, one observes, at a considerable distance preceding the *agni*, a *b* associated with five digits, collateral to and as it were insistent on itself, quite in the manner of what has been noticed, as the sub-virgular Ogham at Killeen Cormac. The digits, however, seem to me to be natural *rugæ* of the surface to which the *b* has been accommodated. Here we perceive a little lapidary rebus of *b* " *o* " (from) *n*, which, with the *agni* following, make up the name of Bonagnus, Bonán, the founder and giver of its name to the original church. The rest of the legend appears to be Bonan's pedigree to his great, great, great grandfather, omitting the intermediate *maqi's*. I would read it as Bonan, son of Adlon, son of Nireman, son of Esscu, son of Lamidan, son of Dangon, terminating with *Maqi Mucoi*. But the modest names enumerated present a much more pompous appearance in their amplified Oghamic forms—

$$B[ON]AGNiMA[Q]IHADDIL_E^ONA$$
$$NIReMNAQAGNIESSICONIDDALA$$
$$NG_U^ONIMU_T^COI \qquad LAMIT_O^AIDAGNI$$

b(o)nagni maqi haddilona niremnaqagni essiconi
ddalangoni mucoi lamitaidagni,

being, I believe, the longest inscription in legible Ogham letters yet found. The *maqi mucoi* at the end appears to show that

these words here, as in previous examples, are not part of the RESIDUE OF
pedigree, but something extrinsic and formal. If they be so KERRY.
here, it is difficult to see why they should not be so considered
where interjected into other legends. I cannot but think
that, as I imagine is the case in the *maqi decceda* example
also, the words relate to our Lord, and correspond to pious
formulas thrown in at the end of other inscriptional legends,
as in the biliteral Roman and Runic carving at Vinge, West
Gothland, where, between the Latin at one side, and its Norse
echo at the other, are interjected the words *Ave Maria Gratia.*
But this is only my guess, and must be taken for what it may
hereafter appear to be worth.

180. In the same parish, from a rath-cave in the townland
of Laharan, two inscribed pillar-stones were many years ago *Laharan*
dug up, and utilised in the walls of a neighbouring dwelling. 57
They have been removed thence, and now form part of the *u. l.*
Earl of Dunraven's collection at Adare Manor. The first is
read by Mr. Brash—

Maqi ritta maqi colabot.   (A)

The second, inscribed on two arrises, appears to repeat the
last name, which, it will be remembered, Mr. Brash also finds
at Kiltera, in Waterford—

Left arris—   *Coillabottas mqi corbi.*   (B)
Right „   *Maqi mucoi qcooi.*

(Og. Mon., 222.)

181. At Adare Manor, probably derived from this region, is
another monument bearing the legend in Ogham, according
to Mr. Du Noyer's drawing (MS., R.I.A.), confirmed by Lord
Dunraven in the " Memorials of Adare"—

Corbagni maqi bifata.   (C)

182. An open, cheerful country extends from Kilbonane,
westward to the sea. Overlooking the sands of the Bay of
Castlemaine, about midway between Killorglin and Milltown,
are the lands of Tinnahally, with their rath and its cave, *Tinnahally*
which has furnished two very fine examples of Ogham to 57
the Museum of the Academy. The first, a huge rude block, *u. l.*

RESIDUE OF KERRY.

presents X, evidently in its *ea* power, as coming between consonants, in the legend—

Anm teagan maqi deglen,

where all signs of inflection have disappeared, arguing comparatively a late date. It is the last *anm* which we meet with. The formula is peculiar to the south and south-west of Ireland. I would, with Haigh, imagine it practically equivalent to the "titulus" or "jacet" of the Welsh Romanesque inscriptions, and that, literally, it means "the name of" the person commemorated. The Bishop of Limerick conceives that it is a contraction for "pro anima," and equivalent to the Patrician formula *oroit do*, "a prayer for the soul of."

Tinnahally

183. The second is a very fine obeliscal pillar, exhibiting a marked example of that kind of double reading already noticed. It has the tenor—

(B)

Anmcfaruddrann Maqi (with strong digits over, very delicately protracted under, the line)—

162.

do ligeinn.

Son of Reading is an Irishism for scholar, or man of learning. Son of two Readings, if this were so rendered, might signify a doctor in both laws. Son of Doligen seems strange to the eye as a patronymic; and, if the early church in this region possessed formulas so peculiar in sepulchral composition, its colleges probably had equally peculiar designations for their grades in learning. However this may be, the *q*, beyond question, is made to serve as a double element in *Maqi* and *Mari.*

Ardywanig
47
l. r.

184. Between Milltown and Castlemaine, at Ardywanig, in the parish of Kilnanare, stands a fine pillar-stone, which in Mr. Windele's time bore an Ogham legend, read by him—

Coftat.

The whole of the inscription has since been split off by the imprudent kindling of a fire against the stone. The addition of one digit to Mr. Windele's sketch would yield the more probable reversed reading—

Festos.

This appears to be the *Ardovenagh* monument on which Mr. RESIDUE OF Windele found, besides the above inscription, a cross inscribed KERRY. in a circle (Og. Mon., 111).

185. Crossing the Castlemaine river and turning westward under the declivities of Slieve Mish, we reach the site of another rath and rath cave at Keel, in the parish of Killgarry-lander. The cave contained a fine inscribed pillar, now at the neighbouring residence of Mr. Rea, at Corkaboy. It is *Corkaboy* inscribed on two angles, one legend terminating and the 46 other beginning on the top where they overlap. The first *l. r.* is—

CATTUFFIQQMAQIRITTE
Cattuffiqq maqi ritte.

The beginning of the second is obscure; it proceeds down the alternate arris—

[iafi]CASMUCOIALLATO
cas mucoi allato,

in reference to which last name, and, indeed, to many of the names with which we have had to deal in this region, I may observe that they are not found in other parts, either of Ireland or Britain, and indicate the presence of a very peculiar and isolated community.

Here, at Corkaboy, we are again under the precipitous sides of Cahir Conree, whence we set out on the Oghamic circuit of Ireland now completed; and, looking back on all that has been, so far, observed, may pause on some of the more obvious generalisations.

First, then, we will, I think, be impressed with the generally Christian character of these monuments; next, with the distinctive character of that Christianity which they represent; and, thirdly, with the evidences of a popular repugnance towards it, taking its rise sometime after the sixth century and manifesting itself down to the present time. We will be inclined, I think, to ascribe more weight to the Irish tradition of a pre-Patrician church than has latterly been accorded to it; and, while regarding Declan, Ibar, Ailbe, and Ciaran, as chronologically following rather than preceding Patrick, will not be indisposed to regard them as representatives rather than

RESIDUE OF
KERRY.

creators of the body of Christians who dwelt south of Slieve
Cua, and into whose bounds neither Palladius, nor Patrick
son of Calphurn, ever penetrated. A review of what
remains in Ogham lapidary work in Britain may perhaps
enable us to take clearer, as they will be wider, views; and I
propose in my next lecture to take up the subject in Wales
and South England.

CHAPTER VI.

The British Oghams frequently accompanied by Roman epigraphs—The Laughar Ogham in Wales, inscribed on base of Roman altar—Bi-lingual inscriptions at Cwm Gloyn, Usk Park, Treffgarn—Pillar stones at St Dogmael's, Llanfechan, Clydai, Cilgerran, Ruthin—Ogham-inscribed stones in Devon—That at Tavistock brought from Roborough Down, near Buckland-Monachorum—Fardel stone now in British Museum—Welsh Oghams at Llandawke, Trallong, Dugoed, Llanwinio, now at Middleton Hall—Bi-lingual stone on Caldey Island—Pillar stones at Bridell, Kenfigg, near Pyle—Sculptured figure on Llywell stone, now in British Museum, compared with that on the Maen Achwnfaen, near Mostyn, in Flintshire.

186. THE Oghams of Britain, although much less numerous than those of Ireland, have, in almost every instance, the great advantage of being accompanied by Roman epigraphs of which they generally are found to be echoes. It may, therefore, be affirmed that they belong to a period subsequent to B.C. 56, and some of them, at least, may, on reasonable grounds, be referred to the period of Roman occupation ending in A.D. 410. Of these latter, the most remarkable is that inscribed on one angle of the base of the Roman altar preserved at Laughar, in Glamorganshire. There is no doubt of the genuine character of the altar. Neither can there be any question that the characters are true Ogham, although the letters *l* and *c*, with indistinct traces of some vowel notches, are all that can now be recognised. If a contemporary inscription, it puts the use of Ogham in Britain back into the time of surviving Paganism, and greatly impairs the argument for its Christian origin; and it would be a somewhat forced assumption to say that it has been added by a later hand. Conjectures of this kind have been employed to rebut the presumption that Oghamic monuments marked with the cross belong to Christian times. If these be, as I conceive they are, inadmissible, much more so would be the employment, as here, of a legend not having any Christian significance to sanctify a relic of Pagan worship. The

WALES.

The Oghams of Britain often accompanied by Roman epigraphs.

Laughar.

I

Laughar altar would, therefore, in any large examination of the question, be provisionally regarded as a self-evidencing Oghamic relic of the Pagan period. It is also, with one exception, the only British Ogham unaccompanied by a Roman context.

187. These contexts vary in their style of writing from well-shaped Roman capitals to mixed capitals and minuscules of the most corrupt forms. The comparative age of the monuments has usually been estimated as proportionate to the less or greater rudeness of the lettering. Imperfection, however, is incident to the beginnings of imitation of newly-set examples, as well as to the withdrawal of their supply; and where other *indicia* exist from which reasonable inferences may be drawn, the palæographic argument may have to be accommodated to them.

188. Such *indicia* are afforded very persuasively by what is called the Vitalianus inscription at Cwm Gloyn, near Nevern, Pembrokeshire. The Ogham merely expresses the name *Fitaliani*. The Roman epigraph is *Vitaliani Emerito*, importing, it seems to me, however ungrammatically, that Vitalian was an *emeritus* or retired military servant of the Empire.

189. The same may be said of the Usk Park inscription, Crickhowel, Breconshire. It is conceived in a Latin taste quite different from the crude Christian Oghamic formula—

Turpilli ic iacit pueri triluni dunocati,

echoed in part by the Ogham which employs X for the exceptional *p*, *Turpili*, and after a long lacuna two *n's*. I take "triluni" to have reference to the child's life of three months. If a proper name, the epigraph would lose something of its Latin aspect, but the *p* of Turpill and the "pueri" would still distinguish it from the other biliterals of what may be called mere British origin, and point to a dominant Roman influence in the composition. Nevertheless, it is to be observed that *Turpill* is put in the genitive, as in the Irish example, though, perhaps, the following *ic iacit* may be meant to be taken in the concrete, corresponding to a suppressed *lapis* or *titulus*.

190. The *Hogtivis* inscription at Little Treffgarn, south of

Fishguard, Pembrokeshire, may also, I would suppose, be WALES. referred to the same period. The Latin legend is—

Hogtivis filius Demeti.

The *H* is used as in regular Latinity, not for *N*, as in later examples. That the name is Hogtivis (seemingly a British corruption of Octavius), is manifested by the accompanying Ogham, which, however, carries it a step further away from the original by presenting it in the coarse form

HUGTIFFS.

All the Roman characters are capitals, although of very rude execution.

191. Were we to judge solely by the form of the letters and their less or greater departure from the Roman model, we might refer to about the same period the pillar-stone at St. Dogmael's, near Cardigan, vouched in all dissertations on *St. Dogmael's.* Oghamic writing, as the primary evidence for the equivalency of *Maqi* to the Latin *Filii.* It is a monument of some elegance, considering that, like all the class, it is untouched by any other tool but the graver. It is also the first, so far noticed in this section, which stands in an ecclesiastical cemetery, and may reasonably be taken as Christian, although not having any distinctive emblem. The

Sagrani fili Cunotami

of the Latin, running down the face of the stone, is echoed with some small variations, in

Sagramni maqi Cunatami

of the Ogham running up its angle, in the usual course. Sagran and Cunotam (doubtless the Welsh Cyndaf) I would imagine to be, both, British names.

192. A more rudely-executed legend, marked also by a debased form of the Latin G, although still employing the regular E instead of the Hiberno-Saxon form of that letter, from the church of Llan Vaughan or Llanfechan, in Car- *Llanfechan.* marthenshire, may belong to the same category. It commemorates Trengad, son of Maclan, as these names would probably appear to us if presented in their secular undress. The Latin text is

Trenacatus ic iacit filius maglagni.

The Ogham accompaniment, very clearly cut, expresses only

Trenaccattlo,

where *lo* remains, so far as I understand, unexplained, if it be not the early British representation of the Gaulish *loga*.

193. The transition from the regular Roman R to the form now regarded as the Irish and Hiberno-Saxon variety appears to have begun at the date of the next monument to be noticed. This also stands in consecrated ground in the churchyard of Clydai, near Newcastle Emlyn, in Cardigan-shire. Although the top of the pillar has been cut off to form the seat for a sun-dial, the whole of the Latin and enough of the associated Ogham to show that it was an echo, remains;

Newcastle Emlyn.

eterni fili victor
ETTERN —— TOR

together expressing the name of Ettern, son of Victor. The name Ettern, Eddern, Edeyrn, is Brito-Latin, as Victor is purely so, and both may well be taken as of, or soon after, the Occupation period. A most attractive theory regarding this inscription has been put forward by Haigh. He took it for a monument raised by the Emperor Flavius Victor to his uncle Eternalis, both well-evidenced historic persons. But the obstacle of the *fili* seems to be insuperable.

Cilgerran. **194.** In the same district, at Cilgerran, on the Teivy, in the parish cemetery, stands the pillar of Trengus. Its Latin legend is

Trenegussi fili Macutreni hic iacit.

It bears a double cross, but apparently not of contemporaneous execution or design. An Ogham has once existed down all the length of one arris, seemingly, from what remains, expressing the names *Trengus* and *Maqitreni*.

195. So far all these indeterminate Welsh monuments, of which it can only be predicated that they are of Roman but not demonstrably of Christian times, are found in South

Wales. One Ogham inscribed monument only has been hitherto found in North Wales, and it belongs to the same category. It stands in Pool Park near Ruthin, Monmouthshire, and bears, in well-shaped, though greatly worn, Roman characters, what seems to be the name Amilini with his designation *Tovisaci* (W. tywysog, Ir. " Toisech " or chief) superadded, and this is echoed by an Ogham on the face of the stone where Tosech takes the form *tofisac*.

196. Besides these, are still two other British examples found, not in Wales, but in South England, belonging to the same category. Both come from the district of Devonshire, bordering on Exmoor. The first, now preserved at the Rectory, Tavistock, originally stood on Roborough Down, near Buckland Monachorum. Like the *Tovisaci* example, it adds to the name of the person commemorated his designation or calling.

Dobuni fabri fili Enabarri,

on the flat, echoed by

Enabarr

in Ogham characters, now much worn but still legible, along the edge of the stone. Enbar would appear as Celtic a form of name as Finbar or Cathbar; and its occurrence so far eastward of Wales and Cornwall cannot but be historically interesting.

197. From the same region, north of Ivybridge, comes the better known Fardel monument, now in the British Museum. The

Fanoni Maquirini

of its Roman epigraph is accompanied by an Ogham expressing the singular sounds

$$SFAQQ_U^O QA_S^C$$

MAQIQICI.

Sfaqqucci Maqi Qici.

We have, however, met *Sfaqqucci* before in the less repulsive form of *Saffiqegi* of the Dunbell, Kilkenny, monument. It and *Qici* probably designate *Fanon* and *Quirin* by their equivalents in Ogham nomenclature. The coarseness of the sounds grates on ears accustomed to the ordinary harmonies of our language. Those uncouth designations may,

DEVON, WALES. however, have been adopted as evidence of self-disparagement by some Christian ascetic. The Celtic sounding *Sagran* in its ceremonial form *Sagramni* appears on the back of the stone. The letters are more in the Irish or Hiberno-Saxon taste than on the other examples above noticed ; and altogether the aspect of the monument is suggestive of Irish and Christian associations.

Llandawke. **198.** A strong savour of Christian times and Irish association also distinguishes a Welsh Ogham monument at Llandawke Church, near Lougharne, in Pembrokeshire, although not marked with any symbol. The Latin inscription on the flat reads *Barrivendi Filius Vendubari*, and on one edge *Hic iacit*, all in not unshapely capitals, save that the *s* of Filius is reversed. On both edges there are Oghams, which, read in the ordinary reverse course to the Latin, yield at one side

$$\text{HUMELEDONA}^{\text{S}}_{\text{F}}$$

and at the other *Maqi M(ucoi)*. A fracture of the top of the stone leaves us uncertain of what should follow ; but the space which has been occupied suggests the formula *Mucoi*. Here again we may reasonably conjecture that *Humeldons* is the Oghamic *alias* of Barrfind, son of Findbar, as the subject of the memorial would, I imagine, have been called in the vernacular of his day, and may add this as a further example of *Mucoi* terminal.

Trallong. **199.** So far, however probable the Christian origin of the monuments enumerated, or some of them, may be, we have nothing amounting to demonstrative proof. But when the cross forms part of the composition, the presumption of its Christian origin cannot be rejected. The cross-signed Ogham monuments of Wales are hardly less numerous than those not so distinguished, and in the palæographic point of view may claim an equal antiquity. At Trallong, between Crickhowel and Brecon, there is preserved in connection with the parish church one of these obviously Christian memorials, remarkable for the comparative elegance of its Roman lettering, and for the clean-cut indisputable completeness of the accompanying Ogham ; and for a phrase of the Ogham formula still unexplained. The Latin legend is

Cumocenni Filius Cunoceni Hic iacit, and the Ogham *Cunacenna* WALES.
fiil ffeto. Cunocenn or Cunacenn, has become Cyngen, as in
Ireland it formerly was Concon. It is obviously the patron-
nymic from which the Concani of Ptolemy took their tribe-
name, and it need be no surprise to find it anywhere in Celtic
Western Europe at any time from the earliest ages. This
Cyngen or Concon will be readily recognised as one of the
earlier British Christians; but we cannot so readily see how
the Ogham *fiil ffeto* corresponds as it ought to do to the
filius hic jacet of the Latin. *Fiil* may be *fili*, transposed by
oversight or pedantry of the carver; but *Ffeto*, as an
equivalent for *jacet*, introduces us to a new verb, which, in
Ogham, is more than the discovery of a new species, or even
a genus in Natural History.

200. The same neighbourhood which yields the *Etterni*
stone, supplies another cross-signed Ogham monument at the
farm of Dugoed. It is a Maltese cross in a circle, having a *Dugoed.*
double line below, which appears to have served at once as a
support to the cross and a stem-line for Ogham characters.
Besides these there is an Ogham inscription along the arris,
which reads

$$\text{DOFT}^{\text{A}}_{\text{O}}\text{C}^{\text{OO}}_{\text{E}}\text{S}$$

and gives the key to the proper name *Dob* [   ]
filius Evolengi in the Roman epigraph. Here we are
reminded of Corpmac, otherwise *Evolengus*, the Eolang
and Olan of Aghabulloge. A singularly - complicated
ligature following the *Dob*—and taking in some members of
the Filius—may contain all the letters for completing
Dobtageos; and digits, which formerly existed along the
line of the cross's stem, may have completed the Ogham echo
of both names. But between what remains of the Roman
and of the Oghamic lettering, each supplanting the other,
Duftac, son of Evoleng, has, on this stone, had his name and
his faith commemorated as long, perhaps, as any other British
or Irish Christian.

201. From Llanwinio, on the borders of Carmarthenshire
and Pembrokeshire, there has been brought to Middleton *Middleton*
Hall, near Llandeilo, a cross-signed bi-literal monument of *Hall.*

WALES. exceptional interest, on account of the form taken by the Ogham equivalent for the Latin *avi*, used seemingly in the sense of "descendant of," like the Irish *uaibh*, "de nepotibus," now the common patronymical *O*. The Llanwinio stone offers a singular example of Roman characters more difficult to read than their accompanying Oghams. This arises from the employment of ligatures, and also, I imagine, from a tampering with one letter. The first line, containing the principal name, has hitherto been read BIAD—. The cast shows a ligature of the A, thus ＶＡ, equivalent to LVA. The supposed B I take to be S. The cast also shows the supposed D as H with its lower section rounded into D. H is the Irish form of N in Welsh inscriptions. Taking it so, the abnormal-looking *Biadi* disappears, and its place is taken by the more recognisable *Silvani*. Then follows AVIBOGIBEVE, where a singularly-shaped G might leave us in further doubt, were it not that the accompanying Ogham reads plainly *affi boci* at one side, and BEFfE at the other. It omits the principal name; otherwise Silvanus would have been earlier detected. The value of the text lies in the AVI, which both here and in the Irish examples appears to signify "grandson"—but of whom? *Bogibeve* is not a likely name. Mr. Haigh, in the essay referred to, by a careful analysis of all the Welsh inscriptional formulas, shows good ground for taking *Bogus* as the grandfather and *Beve* as the name of the person erecting the monument. The Ogham confirms his reasoning, showing *affiboci* and *beffe* separately and in reverse courses of reading. A cross inscribed in an oval occupies the head of the stone.

202. In all these cases the cross forms an integral part of the design; but there is one cross-signed Oghamic monument on which the Ogham certainly appears to have existed before its Latin legend and sculptured crosses. This is the Caldey *Caldey Island* inscription. It is now deposited in the church on Caldey island, Pembrokeshire. It bears the well-known Latin inscription beseeching of the passers-by a prayer for the soul of *Catuocon*, which, if it be not an early Cadogan, may, like the *Olacon* of Ballynesturig, stand for some *Cathcu* who had carried that warlike name to this peaceful hermitage off the rocks of Tenby. The lettering is very Irish in all its characteristics.

But, what is strange, it commences with *et*, as if in continua- WALES
tion of something preceding; and, while the stone was built
into the wall of the church porch, antiquaries hoped for the
missing sentences on the back, and speculated on the traces
of Ogham digits near the top as probably being in continuation of others on the concealed arrises. The removal of the
stone has shown these speculations to be groundless. The
Ogham is merely a fragment, the top having been broken off,
and quite illegible. But what is worthy of note is, that while
the Latin letters are deep-cut and sharp in every outline,
the Ogham digits and notches are so worn and abraded that
no one looking at the monument could suppose them contemporaneous, and the engraver of Catuocon's prayer has
evidently regarded them as immaterial, two of his crosses on
the upper sides of the slab being cut through and over the
attenuated traces of some of them. It is indeed a palim-
psest in stone; but the original, which it is hard to think
even of the early Christian period, is irrecoverable. They
have been read as yielding a sequence of vocables, but I am
unable to follow it, and offer no transliteration.

203. Reverting to the rich Oghamic tract of Cardiganshire,
which has already furnished the Clydai and Dugoed examples,
I would now refer to the neighbouring parish of Bridell. *Bridell stone.*
Here a great pillar of stone, worthy to compare with some of
the Irish examples, stands in the churchyard. It bears a
quatrefoil cross in a circle on one side, and an unusually
long Ogham legend along the angle. It, however, possesses
no other inscription by which the transliteration or construing
of its Ogham might be helped; and the disintegration of its
lichen-covered surface makes the determination of their values
extremely difficult. The legend begins near the bottom with
the group *Netta Sagri*, or *Nettasagruma*. The difference
depends on whether one indentation is a vowel notch or a
natural flaw. In any case we recognise the Irish *Netta*.
Then follows *Maqi Mucoi greci* or *breci*, depending on whether
six or seven scores have been employed at the top. I have
no doubt there are seven, and all cross the line. Whether it
be *breci* or *greci*, the matter of chief interest is the occurrence
here of the frequent Irish formula *Maqi mucoi*. It is to Mr.

Brash I am indebted for correcting an erroneous reading of my own in this group of digits, which I had imagined contained the name of a Bishop Oudoc. The only criterion for the age of the monument is the style of the Ogham lettering, which employs both short digits and notches for vowels, and may, I think, be therefore regarded as among the latest of the Welsh Ogham monuments.

204. Still, what should be deemed late, and what early, rests in the utmost vagueness, unless some time can be fixed before or after which there may be reasonable ground for supposing some of those inscriptions to have been executed, and there remain two of them which may, I think, justify some speculation more or less confident in that *Kenfigg stone* direction. These are the Kenfigg and the Llywell monu-
at Pyle. ments. The Kenfigg stone, standing by the high-road from Pyle to Margam, in Glamorganshire, bears a Roman inscription down its face, with Ogham characters on its adjoining side arrises. The top arris I would say, from careful examination, has never borne any inscription. The surface, with its natural pittings and rugosities, bears no appearance of having anywhere been smoothed or abraded, and is free from the least trace of artificial sculpture. The Latin epigraph, it is agreed on all hands, is *Pumpeius Carantorius.* The *e* is of the Irish or Hiberno-Saxon form, ᴇ, being, with one exception, the only instance in which the Roman epigraphs associated with these Welsh Oghams exhibit the late Irish influence. Its presence would seem to me to denote a period when personages bearing Roman names of distinction were no longer resident in Britain, and to show that Ogham writing and the word *maqi* for " son " lingered in Britain at least until after the Irish character had been partly adopted into lapidary writing. The Bishop of Limerick, I would think, has hardly allowed time for its adoption into British lapidary writing when he seeks to find here the name of Saint Carentoc of the sixth century, though he was the son of Pompa; and Pompa, in the form Popa, may possibly be spelled in one section of the Ogham. It would be a very welcome standing-ground for this Welsh exploration if one could accept this identification

as unreservedly as that of St. Olan. But I confess I regard the characters taken as *p p* in the Ogham group to the right as symbols, not letters. They are tri-radial groups corresponding to the alleged old Welsh symbol of the Trinity. The received opinion of late years has been that the symbol is of modern origin. I am bound to say I do not think so. If I do not deceive myself, it exists on the Hayle inscription in Cornwall, associated with a Roman *in pace*. Everything at this side I take to be symbolical, and believe it a fair question whether, with their accompanying groups of vowels, there be not here three such tri-radial characters; and, regarding these associated vowels, I will further own that I do not consider the statement of there having been a vocalic equivalent for the tri-radial symbol as by any means a bardic imposture. One limb of one of these symbols is protracted across the line, and, if it stood alone, would form *m*. On the opposite side — and we may remember the examples of detached initials, already noticed — are the remains of a lengthy Ogham inscription, extending from the top to the ground. We can recognise *erl* and, after abraded vowel places, digits which may be the remains of *ng*, followed, after other abrasions, by *n maqi ll*, and this, after a further lacuna, by *na*, all which contain in their proper sequence the essential parts of the legend—

(M)erl(i)ng(i a)nmaq(i)ll(ia)na.
Merlingi   anmaqi   lliana.

The designation of Merlin in Welsh tradition is *an map lliana*, or the misborn son of the nun. He was the child without a father of the legend of Vortigern, as old at least as the tenth century, and the very head of Welsh esoteric mystical doctrine. I do not suppose that this is his grave, but I submit that the monument is later than the story of the son of the Nun of Carmarthen who confounded the Druids of Vortigern, and that we must consider Ogham writing and the formula *maqi* to have survived in Wales down at least to some time after his era.

205. At the other terminus of the inquiry, the Llywell *Llywell stone.* stone will supply matter for a good deal of reflection. It was found, I believe, at a place near Trecastle, in Brecon-shire, called Pant y Cadno, and is now in the British Museum, and is charged, face, back, and one arris, with inscriptional work. A Roman legend runs up the back, echoed by an Ogham one running down the arris, and the face of the stone is covered down to the ground-line with ornamentation and barbaric imagery, and possibly something more. The Roman characters are slightly debased capitals. The only uncertain-ties are whether the first letter is M or V, and whether the sixth letter from the bottom is a C or a debased G. To my eye the initial is V and the other G, yielding the reading—

Vaccutreniimaqisaligiduni.

It is the only instance of a Latin *maqi*, and appears to com-memorate Maccutren son of Salgin or Sulgen, and is echoed by the shorter Ogham—

Maqitrenii salicidni.

Maccutrenus is already familiar to us, and may be Irish or British-Celtic. Sulgen is Welsh, and, I would suppose, may equally be Irish. Let us now turn to the face. It is some-what wider at top. Horizontal lines divide it into four panels, under the lowermost of which the surface is left untouched, for insertion in the ground. Being so inserted, the first section of the Roman and the concluding section of the Ogham inscription are buried out of sight, leaving the panelled face in full view. The first thing that strikes one is, that here is a kind of barbaric ornamentation very much in the style of the Irish Pagan monuments. But that the work is Christian is evinced by crosses introduced at either side of a figure represented as trampling on a serpent in the third panel. The extraordinary rudeness of this figure—which consists merely of a circle with dots for the head, two lines diverging below for the limbs and feet, and two for the arms, there being no body—would make one hesitate in ascribing any intelligible meaning to it, were it not that the figure on the lower front panel of the sculptured cross called the Maen Achwnfaen, near Mostyn, in Flintshire, engaged in similar action, gives a key to the sculptor's intention. The Flintshire figure itself is barbarous in a high degree, but

Figure on the Llywell stone, compared with one on the Maen Achwn-faen, a sculp-tured cross near Mostyn.

exhibits a body and limbs contained within outlines, and WALES. expresses, with a good deal of spirit, trampling action. It is unnecessary here to inquire whether it be a spear it grasps in one hand or the tail of the serpent. It must be accepted as a remarkable instance of the possible combination of very good art in ornamentation (for this is one of the most elaborately-designed and decorated of all the British crosses) with extremely low ideas in the drawing of the human figure. The being who tramples on the serpent, however, in the Flintshire example, is well pictured in comparison with the corresponding figure on this Breconshire pillar-stone. Another attempt to represent a bishop with his pastoral staff on the panel below is equally infantile and excessively grotesque. A dotted circle for the head, two lines, divergent below, for the limbs and feet; two lines, one of them branching in three at the extremity, for the arms and a hand; and another for the curved-headed crozier, constitute this second figure, the general effect of which is singularly like the barbaric imagery of some of the Loughcrew monuments. The accessories are altogether in the taste of the Irish Pagan monuments—flowing zig-zags, concentric curves, and rows of short parallel straight lines insistent on and dependent from others. A third intimation of a human figure appears at one side of the top, having near it a shield-like object, inscribed with a St. Andrew's cross. The next panel below, charged with a complication of curves and reticulations, is traversed by a strongly-incised tri-radial device issuing from above. In this it is difficult not to recognise the same object employed on the Kenfigg monument. It is followed, on the panel below, by a catena of ten lunette-shaped characters resembling the four *Coll* Ogham digits which stand for the vowel *e* in the Kilbonane legend. There are ten of these, which, as Oghams, would yield the vowels *o*, *i*, *u*. It was intimated in commenting on the Kenfigg stone, that certain vowel groups have been alleged to have a known relation to this tri-radial figure. They express, according to modern Welsh bardism, the mystery of the Trinity and the Divine name. In the language of the Barddas, the voice in which God declared Himself "had in it the utterance of the three notes corresponding to the three rays.—Thus was the voice that was heard placed on record in the symbol.—The sense of O was given to the first column, the sense of I to the second or middle column, and the sense of V to the third—It was thus that God declared His name and existence, $\underset{\text{OIV}}{\text{Ꝥ}}$." The writer vouches no authority for what he alleges older than that of Welsh mystical writers of the fifteenth and seventeenth centuries, and the tri-radial symbol and its vocalic exponent have been generally rejected by modern scholars, as late and dishonest inventions. These lapidary evidences, however, give the subject a new aspect, and it may be worth while in their presence to recur to the words of one of the Welsh writers, vouched by *Ab Ithel*, Davydd Nanmor, who died A.D. 1460, in reference to our Lord—

> O. i. ag W. yu ag Oen.
> He is O. I. & W., and a Lamb.

To which it may be added that the same authorities allege the original O. I. V. (which would be ·· ····· ··· Oghamically) was prior to the time of Taliesin written, as ten *Coll* Oghams are capable of being sounded, O. I. O.—(*Barddas*, p. 65.)

This catena is followed by the remains of what appear to have been alphabetic characters, and by digits in all respects similar to those which, on Breton and Norse rock carvings have hitherto been taken for boats with their crews, here inverted. They are identical with the objects seen on the sculptured sepulchral slabs of the Irish Pagan tumuli at Loughcrew. If they be real links between the digit and notch Ogham of this class of monuments, and the fantastic sculpturings of the Pagan tombs of Ireland, the field of inscriptional inquiry would acquire vastly-enlarged bounds, and a new and extraordinary literary interest; but everything is so wild and disorderly on the Irish Pagan sculptures, that the prospect of eliciting material for any tangible comparison is extremely remote. One cannot, however, look on these survivals of the Pagan taste, intermingling with the first efforts of art in Christian symbolism, without a strong conviction that the monument belongs to the very earliest age of Christianity in Britain, and that the much- discredited date of the end of the second century for the mission of *Fagan* and *Dubric* looks less improbable in the light of this lapidary record from the country of the Silures.

206. During this examination of Welsh monuments, ranging probably from the third or fourth, and coming down, it may be, to the sixth or seventh century, a statement in Cormac's Glossary respecting the Welshmen who accompanied Patrick to Ireland, already referred to in connection with Irish examples supplementing the ordinary Ogham alphabet with an exceptional character for the letter P, will often have recurred to the mind :—

"CRUIMTHER, i.e , the Gaelic of *presbyter*. In Welsh it is *premter* : *prem*, 'worm,' in the Welsh is *cruim* in the Gaelic. *Cruimther*, then, is not a correct change of *presbyter* · but it is a correct change of *premter*. The Britons, then, who were in attendance on Patrick when preaching were they who made the change, and it is *primter* that they changed ; and accordingly the literati of the Britons explained it, i e as the worm is bare, sic decet presbyterum, who is bare of sins and quite naked of the world, &c., secundum eum qui dixit ego [autem] sum vermis [Ps. xxii. 6 : ataimse conad cruim me 7 nach duine B], &c."

If this *mac* was *map*, it is difficult to understand how it comes that the formulas in use in these inscriptions are *maqi*, *maccu*, and that so many of the proper names are Irish in aspect, unless on the theory of an Irish Celtic occupation of those parts of Wales and South Britain in which the monuments are found. The fact of some kind of occupation by Irish Celts, whether by conquest or friendly settlement, during the second or third century, and thenceforward till their expulsion about the close of the sixth, is very strongly attested both by Welsh and Irish authority of a high antiquity. Whether Nennius, or the continuator of Nennius, be the author, an Irish settlement of the sons of Liathan in South Wales is one of the oldest British historical events on native record. The Irish annalists allege an extended dominion over Britain, by which probably we are to understand, Wales and Cornwall, in and subsequent to the reign of Criffan, son of Fidach, A.D. 360. Cormac's Glossary carries back the Welsh and South British intercourse to an earlier period. The historic genuineness of the tradition may be inferred from its being given in the Glossary as incidental to a comparatively trivial story of the importation of the first lapdog into Ireland. Testimonies given thus undesignedly are free from the suspicion of being fabricated for an historical purpose. The entry under the heading *Mug éime*, slave of the hilt, is as follows :—

" *Mug-Éime*, that is the name of the first lapdog that was in Ireland. Cairbre Musc, son of Conaire (1) brought it from the east from Britain ; for when great was the power of the Gael on Britain, they divided Alba between them into districts, and each knew the residence of his friend, and not less did the Gael dwell on the east side of the sea quam in Scotica, and their habitations and royal forts were built there. Inde dicitur *Dinn Tradui*, i.e., Triple-fossed Fort, of Crimthann the Great, son of Fidach (2), King of Ireland and Alba to the Ictian sea (3). It is there was Glass son of Cass, Swineherd of the King of Hiruaith (4), with his swine feeding, and it was he that Patrick resuscitated at the end of six score (a) years after he was slain by the soldiers of Mac Con. And it is in that part of Dinn map Lethain in the lands of the Cornish Britons, i.e., the Fort of Mac Liathain, for *mac* is the same as *map* in the British. Thus every tribe divided on that side (b), for its property to the east was equal [to that on the west] (c), and they continued in this power till long after the coming of Patrick. Hence Cairbre Musc was visiting in the East his family and his friends. At this time no lapdog had come into the land of Eirin, and the Britons commanded that no lapdog should be given to the Gael on solicitation or by free will, for gratitude or friendship. Now at this time the law among the Britons was, ' Every criminal for his crime such as breaks the law ' (a). There was a beautiful lapdog in the possession of a friend of Cairbre Musc in Britain, and Cairbre got it from him [thus]. Once as Cairbre [went] to his house, he was made welcome to everything save the lapdog. Cairbre Musc had a wonderful skene, around the haft whereof was adornment of silver and gold. It was a precious jewel. Cairbre put much grease about it and rubbed fat meat to its haft, and afterwards left it before the lapdog. The lapdog began and continued to gnaw the haft till morning, and hurt the knife, so that it was not beautiful. On the morrow Cairbre made great complaint of this, and was sorry for it, and demanded justice for it of his friend. ' That is fair indeed : I will pay for the trespass,' said he. ' I will not take aught,' says Cairbre, ' save what is in the law of Britain, namely, " every animal for his crime." ' The lapdog was therefore given to Cairbre, and the name, i.e. *Mug-éime* (slave of a haft) clung to it, from *mug* ' a slave ' [and *éim* <small>WALES.</small> ' a haft '], because it was given on account of the skene. The lapdog (being a bitch) was then with young Ailill Flann the Little (5) was then king over Munster, and Cormac, grandson of Conn (6), at Tara ; and the three took to wrangling, and to demand and contend for the lapdog ; and the way in which the matter was settled between the three of them was this, that the dog should abide for a certain time in the house of each. The dog afterwards littered, and each of them took a pup of her litter, and in this wise descends every lapdog in Ireland still."

It will probably be thought that at this time the presence of the Irish was rather that of peaceful settlers, for the law to which reference is made was Roman law, and a hostile occupation of imperial territory was little likely at this period. If, then, there were an Irish population speaking a language different from that of the native British in these regions at that time, it would appear highly probable that the Irish-sounding formulas and names found on Welsh and South British Ogham inscriptions ought to be ascribed to them. It is indeed very difficult to come to any other conclusion, if it be conceded that in St. Patrick's time the Welsh ecclesiastics could not pronounce *Cruimthir*, but called it *Prempter*. But this depends on whether the Welsh in question were companions of Patrick of Dunbarton, the son of Calphurn, or of Palladius, also called Patrick. There is no doubt that Palladius sailed on his Irish mission attended by numbers of Britons from the port of Menevea, now St. David's, in A.D. 431. If the Britons who accompanied him used *p* for *k*, it would be extremely difficult to treat the *maqis* of the Welsh Oghams as of British origin. But the language of Western and Southern Britain during the time of the Roman occupation, so far as it can be judged of by the names of persons and places and their occasional interpretations in works of early authority, is argued with much force to have been substantially the same as that which may legitimately be supposed to have then been spoken in Ireland ; and the differences which now exist between the Welsh and Irish languages are sought to be accounted for, and not unreasonably, by that Cymric invasion from North Britain of the 6th century led by Cunedda and his eight sons, which British scholars are agreed in accepting as an historical event. To these Britons of Cumbria and Strathclyde from the north, and to subsequent Cymric infusions pouring themselves westward before Anglo-Saxon pressure, the change may be due which, as early as Cormac's time, had made *Mac* Irish, and *Map* Welsh; and assuming Patrick Calphurnides to have been accompanied on his Irish mission by Britons of that Cymric race and language, the statement of Cormac may be referred to him rather than to Palladius, and may well consist with the Welsh claim to be left in possession of their old Ogham monuments.

207. The palæographic difficulty remains. Assume the language of Britain before the epoch of Cunedda to have been the same with that of Ireland. Assume the Cuneddan revolution to have altered it into the language of the now oldest Welsh writings. The *maqi*-bearing Ogham epigraphs must then be referred to the pre-Cuneddan period, during the greater part of which good Roman models were at hand, and the production of letters so debased as we find associated with many of the examples, rendered, in the estimation of scholars, unlikely if not impossible. It may be a question whether scholarship has not overreached itself by excessive scientific nicety, or whether the continuing *maqi* be not hieratic, and a survival of some special school of inscriptional phraseology. This might be supposed in the case of formulas like *maqi* and *maccu*, but that the Irish-sounding names should also have been continued after their Welsh modifications had come into use, seems hard to admit. To the fourth, fifth, and sixth centuries, however, if we accept the theory of an identical speech in Ireland and Britain, we seem coerced to refer the Oghams the subject of this lecture, although associated with epigraphs which we have been taught to regard as two, three, and four centuries later in date. Notwithstanding these difficulties, the inclination of my own mind would be to accept the theory, especially as in the old Irish tradition preserved in the Book of Invasions the *Fid-genta* or people of the woods, the *autochthones* of Ireland are designated Britons. Holding this view, I should be bound to admit that, *cæteris paribus*, a British claim to have imparted this kind of writing to the Irish would rest on reasonable <small>WALES</small> probability. For the Irish were there in as good a position to be receivers of the gift as bestowers of it; the Ogham bases itself on an alphabetic system, having a Latin aspect; and the natural course of transmission of Latin influences would *prima facie* be through Britain to the outer island. But if the Ogham be of British origin, it may be affirmed with confidence that it originated there after the British emigration to Armorica, generally referred to the time of Maximus, 383-9; for, notwithstanding extended special search, no Ogham has ever been found in Brittany or elsewhere on the Continent.

208. But a greater than the palæographic difficulty must still be surmounted before we can say that Ogham was of British as distinguished from Irish origin, or *vice versâ*. On the one hand, we may have been struck, in the Welsh examples, with the absence of scholastic trickeries. On the other, we will have noticed that they almost all present their genitive name-terminations in the Latin *i*; and that such forms as the Irish *ias, as, a ; os, o ;* are absent. Language is distinguished from the other gifts of man in this, that it becomes more perfect, in the sense of having more inflectional forms, as we go back towards its beginnings. These guides to the relations of words undergo a continual process of decay and removal; dropping, first, one syllable, then another, then disappearing altogether. I do not suppose that philology has any means of computing the time necessary for these changes; but, as they are gradual, their successions must cover large spaces of human history. If we try to estimate what time it took the *ias* genitive to shorten into *as* and *a*; or the *i* genitive to recede from the termination, and hide itself in the body of the word, as in *maic* for *maqi*, we shall find ourselves demanding periods long behind the Roman advent, and must, in that case, give the prior use to the place in which these forms are found. But if these be not true inflectional forms, but only pedantic devices of the Irish carvers, the conclusion would be that Ogham writing, after its discontinuance in Wales, went on through several stages of a spurious refinement, in the south of Ireland; and to that conclusion, I acknowledge, my own mind is, at present, the more attracted.

209. The discontinuance of Ogham-writing in Wales seems to correspond in date with the reforms consequent on the mission of Augustine. Both in Wales and Ireland there had been great need of reformation : Gildas has drawn the British half of the picture in very dark colours, but with outlines too indistinct to give us more than an indefinite sense of vice and apostacy. We know also how obscure and intangible are the traces of that early Welsh mysticism which Algernon Herbert, in his Neo-Druidic Heresy, deduces from the ambiguous language of the Bards, but it seems pretty evident that there was something esoteric there; and, indeed, we may unconsciously have already had a sample of it in the Kenfigg inscription. If I have been right in deducing the name Merlin, the Son without human father, from its Ogham, and this have its echo, as we might expect, in sense, if not in sound, in the Roman epigraph, it is quite conceivable that He who, in religious language, by His five wounds gives mankind their saving assurance, may be indicated under the associated Pumpeius Carantorius. The Irish hagiologists are also vague and unsatisfying, but they indicate substantially that there was something much amiss in the Irish Church about the same time. Brigid had prophesied that evil teachers were to come who should overthrow doctrine and seduce almost all men; and her biographer, Cogitosus, declares that when King Ainmire, the reformer of the Bards, called in Gildas to restore ecclesiastical law, all, from the highest to the lowest, had lost the Catholic faith; while St. Hildegard, in her life of Desibode, shows the continuing belief in some great heterodoxy of the Irish of the sixth century by representing them as having, in many cases, turned Jews, and, in many, relapsed into Paganism. In this view of the two Churches—both Ogham-using, and both under orthodox censure—we may, I think, see the causes which in Wales led to the disuse of this kind of writing, and, in Ireland, to the disuse also of the graveyards of the sectaries.

CHAPTER VII.

Scottish Oghams differ from those in Ireland, Wales, and England—Shetland
Oghams; Lunnasting: St. Ninian's: Bressay—Orkney; Burrian, Aberdeenshire;
Newton: Logie: Aboyne—Scoonie stone in Fifeshire—Golspie in Sutherland.

210. ALL the older Oghamic monuments of Ireland, and all Scotland.
those of Wales and South England, so far as they are known
to us, are of the digit and notch kind. The Oghamic monu- *Scottish*
ments of Scotland, on the contrary, are all of what has been *Oghams differ*
from those in
termed the scholastic variety, in which digits constitute *Ireland, Wales,*
vowels as well as consonants, and the notch is unknown. *and England.*
The stem-crossing vocalic groups are distinguished from
consonantal by being vertical to the medial line ; but this is
by no means a general rule. In some instances vowels and
consonants are sloped in reversed directions, and in some
reverse inclinations are given to both classes of letters *inter
se.* The consequence is a range of alternative transliterations
so wide that room can only be found for the most obvious
possible variations in the transliterated texts of this section.
The Scottish Oghams, therefore, agreeably to these views,
may be considered the more modern, and in them we may be
prepared to find more of that studied obscurity which appears
to have originated in the pedantry of later ecclesiastical
scribes. They are about equally distributed over the mainland and the islands. In the latter we find no collateral aid
from associated epigraphs, or, save in one instance, from
definitely intelligible sculpture. On the mainland all the
examples ally themselves with peculiar Picto-Scottish forms
of sculpture, which, for such interpretation as they may
receive, require the fuller preparatory exploration. It
will therefore be more convenient to begin our survey from
the Shetland Islands, the most distant point northward at
which Ogham inscriptions have yet been found; then to
take up the Orkney examples, and reserve those found on

the sculptured stones of Aberdeen, Fifeshire, and Sutherland, for final examination. The first, then, of the Scottish island inscriptions which I shall observe on, is that from Lunnasting, on the mainland of Shetland. It is very clearly, I had almost said elegantly, cut on a smooth flag, which retains the traces of every character. . It is, besides, provided with word-divisions; yet the artist has succeeded in making it one of the obscurest Oghams with which we are acquainted. A cross accompanies it, and a cross designates the commencement. It exhibits one group of *coll* digits, recalling the examples at Kilbonane and Llywell; and, in the initial of the second word, employs a character which, in one of the lists of *sigla* or key alphabets of the Irish Book of Ballymote, is set down for *s*. All its digit-groups are tied, and free from the least doubt as to number or position. The transliteration, however, is singularly repellent—

$$\text{TTUIC}_{\substack{\text{NG}\\ \text{\&c.}}}^{\text{U}}\text{HEATTS}:\text{S}\widetilde{\text{EA}}\text{HHTTANNN}:\text{HCCFF}_{\text{ST}}^{\text{E}}\text{FF}:\text{NEHHTONN}.$$

ttuicuheatts seahhttannn hccffeff nehhtonn.

Tuicuheat might ally itself with the *Toichthec* of other examples, and the legend might commemorate a *sechtain* or septenary of his kindred, amongst whom *Nechton* might be one: but the intermediate collection of digits, *hccffeff*, conveys nothing articulate to the ear, and suggests no meaning to the mind, nor will any alternative antithetical or exchangeable adjustment, so far as I can see, solve the riddle, though, without doubt, the characters, when inscribed, had a meaning for those who had the key.

211. The second Shetland Ogham is from the ecclesiastical site of St. Ninian's. It is imperfect at the commencement, but complete at its ending, and consists of two words at most—

——*esmeqqnann ammoffest.*

The name seems a diminutive of affection, and the predicate has all the look of a superlative in *est*, but further I do not enter on the dangerous field of philology.

212. The third example from Shetland, the Bressay monument, affords further evidence of the Ogham having been in

use among a mixed Celtic and Norse population, and a most Scotland.
welcome and well-assured standing-ground in chronology. I
know not whether to regard the Bishop of Limerick's identification of the St. Olan monument in Ireland or of this record
of the descendants of Naddodd, the discoverer of Iceland, as
the more brilliant critical achievement. It is now nearly
thirty years since Dr. Graves read his paper on the Bressay
Stone before the Royal Irish Academy. Up to that time the
strong presumption was that Celtic forms only should be
looked for. It is not until now that any suspicion of Icelandic
or old English forms of speech being concealed in other
Ogham legends of the Scottish islands has been expressed.
Dr. Graves, however, finding the undoubted sequence *dattrr*
following a proper name in the *s* possessive, at once perceived
the Norse character of the monument, and the direction in
which his search after the names of the persons commemorated should be conducted. The stone is in marked contrast
with the modest slabs described in the preceding paragraphs.
It is of considerable size, covered on both faces with Christian
ecclesiastical sculpturings, set in a symbolical framework
representing the swallowing and disgorgement of Jonah, and
engraved on both edges with Ogham legends. These, notwithstanding some pedantries belonging to the later school of
writing, may be transliterated—

CRROBSCC : NAHHTFFDDADDS : DATTRR : aNN.
ccrroscc nahhtffddadds dattrr an—,

the terminal digits being uncertain ; and—

BENNR^PES : MEQQDDRROI ANN.
bennrres meqq ddrroi ann.

Dr. Graves has pointed out that *ccrroscc* for *crocs* is in harmony
with other Irish examples, and that Nathdod, who discovered
Iceland A.D. 861, had a grandson Benir, to whom if we refer
the Bressay monument, we shall bring the probable age of
this writing to about the middle of the tenth century.

213. I next take up the Orkney example. It comes from *Orkney.*
the Broch (Burgh) or dry-stone round castle of Burrian, in the *Burrian.*
Island of North Ronaldsay, and is now in the National Museum

of the Society of Antiquaries of Scotland. It is a small slab, on the smooth surface of which a cross has been engraved, along with a line of Ogham lettering very delicately cut on an incised stem-line. It is, I fancy, the most minute lapidary Ogham hitherto found. Unfortunately some of its groups are obliterated. It has no division points, and its series of words has to be made out on presumption, and by way of trial. The commencing syllables appear to make a proper name ending in *rrann* or *ragg*. They are followed by groups of digits yielding the sequence *u(u)rract*, which, in a Norse or old English legend, would without difficulty be accepted for "wrought," or "engraved"; after *u(u)rract* comes a combination of digit groups, beginning with the X to which *ea*, *p*, and a possible *th* force have been ascribed, but incapable, as it stands, of yielding any intelligible syllabic sequence. The next and final word begins with angulated digits, which, as Runes, would have the force of *cc*. We are here on the confines of the Norse influence, and may accept these values the more readily because the groups which follow plainly express, with them, *ccrroccs*, "cross." Here, then, are four words, of which the second and fourth are sensible and relevant to the accompanying sculpture, and the first and third, as they stand, insensible. We have had examples of entire legends insensible until inverted, but no evidence as yet of partial inversions of the constituent words. Such, however, would seem to be the key to the Burrian Ogham. The group, illegible as it stood, before *ccrroccs*, turned upside down, becomes *thetts*, "this." For the Burrian legend, therefore, I would submit the transliteration—

(? *rrann*) *uurract thetts ccrroccs.*
(? rrann) wrought (engraved) this cross.

How lapidary writing in Ogham came into Orkney and the Shetlands, may exercise a good deal of speculation. The more obvious idea would be that it had been introduced by the Columban clergy. But the question might be asked with much cogency how it happens that there are no traces of Ogham at Iona, or Derry, or Durrow, or Kells, or at any of the centres of Columban missionary activity on the Continent?

The pre-Columban Christianity of Scotland was that of Gallo- Scotland. way and Strathclyde, and, if we may credit certain legendary statements, which, however, have been generally discredited, an earlier infusion direct from the east into northern Pictland. Galloway and Strathclyde are destitute of Oghams. Pictland alone on the mainland of Scotland possesses them, in like manner as it alone possesses its particular lapidary symbolic sculptures. Pictland, certainly, would be the highway to the Northern Islands and to Iceland, and it may be worth consideration whether the Christian monks called Papæ, whom the discoverers of Iceland found there in the ninth century, were not the representatives of some such pre-Columban influence from the Scottish mainland; for Papa, although it has lingered in the Breton Church, is certainly not Columban nor Irish, but characteristically Eastern.

214. The monument on the mainland of Scotland which in its general aspect most resembles the old Irish and Welsh examples, is that at Newton, in the Garioch, Aberdeenshire. *Newton.* The front of the stone bears an inscription of considerable length in very singular characters, accompanied by a long Ogham legend extending down one side, and having at the lower end a lateral loop not unlike the knot on a Runic worm-band. The loop section has an incised stem-line: the principal line of Ogham follows the drum or natural convexity of the stone where the face rounds into the side. A cross of the filfot kind occurs in the middle of the front inscription, and a cross appears in the Ogham at the front where the collateral digits branch off. It may be thought that no so fantastic forms of letters as those of the principal epigraph have ever been derived from the Roman alphabet. But that opinion will hardly be retained after an inspection of some of the Welsh non-Oghamic lapidary legends, and will, I think, be promptly dismissed in presence of the oak-carved inscriptions of Llanfair Waterdine, Salop. Here, on the chancel-rail of a church of the fourteenth or fifteenth century are two legends in raised characters even more strange to the eye than anything in the Newton epigraph. Yet they are no more than Roman characters and *sigla* pedantically disguised, as appears from the *Maria* with which the first begins, and the words *Esrl flii* concluding the second. These Llanfair texts are adduced, not for the purpose of further elucidating them, which would be beside the present inquiry, but as an instance of the extent to which inscriptional fantasy has gone under Welsh ecclesiastical influences, and as a caution against our allowing the not greater distortions of the Newton text to deter us from seeking their explanation in the alphabet by which we have hitherto found all the British and Irish bi-literal epigraphs explainable. And if the mind be kept from remote and foreign analogies, and prepared to recognise familiar forms, though in glyptical masquerade, the eye, even cursorily glancing over the principal Newton legend, can hardly fail to take in some tangible Latin sequences. In the second line *Furtrin, Rex*; in the third, *Gito ho loco*, with a sign of contraction over the *ho*; in the fourth and fifth, *usscetli fili sitrgsi*; and in the fifth what seem to be ligatures of the component letters of *sepultus*. The name at top is a monogram like the duplex *Cellach* bound up in another set of ligatures. *I, L, T, U*, and *F* are easily distinguishable in each of its two parts. Turning to the Ogham, we experience excessive embarrassment from the absence of any definite stem-line; from the disregard of any distinction between consonantal and vowel groups, it being left uncertain or for ascertainment from the context whether, for example, a group of five digits crossing the *drum* is to be taken for *R* or for *I*; as well as from the probably intentional dropping out of letters and syllables. What presents itself at first sight, including the loop in parenthesis and accepting as a digit a faint indentation to complete the *g* of *regs*, not hitherto taken into account, seems to be—

    uu dd mq qnsn forrennq (regs gist) X *tli.*

This may receive some slight expansion from further accepting a faint underline curved mark after the *q* of *qnsn* for *ui*, and a prolongation of three of the digits of the first *r* into the opposite superior group as equivalent to an inserted *t*, giving—

    udd mq quinsn fotrennq regs gist X *tli,*

yielding, if both ends of the line be taken as reading towards X and the supposed omitted letters be added,

    iltudd m(a)q quins(anti)n fortrennq regs gist.

And certainly the Romanesque monogram, if read like the Scotland. cypher *Cellach* outward from the centre, is quite adaptable to Itudd in the form Iltulf: and Iltulf or Indulf certainly was king of Fortren or Pictland, and was slain A.D. 961, at Inner-colan, in Aberdeenshire, not far north of the Garioch; which would all hang together with reasonable appearance of pro-bability were it not stated, *valeat quantum*, in the Pictish chronicle that Indulf was buried in Iona. I do not attempt to reconcile the discrepancy, but present the reading for what it may be worth, as the only seeming solution to which these lapidary texts conduct.

215. There remain now the four Ogham inscriptions, at Logie and Aboyne, Aberdeenshire; Scoonie in Fife, and Golspie in Sutherland. The Logie ring-Ogham is associated *Logie ring-* with what will, I believe, be shown to be Marian Emblems. *Ogham.* The name Maria contains five letters, and it is made up seemingly of five groups of digits; but there the resemblance ceases. The only vocalisable sequence having any resem-blance to a name which it presents is *Togtuch*, which, if we could be sure of it, might be compared with Toicthech and Toggittac; but the "wheel-Ogham" was cryptic of the cryptic. In the *Amra Coluimkille*, a eulogistic elegy by the bard Dallan Forgaill, the art of reading the "wheel-Ogham" is enumerated among Columba's accomplishments. I fear it has not been transmitted to our times.

216. Neither can I add anything to what is already known of the Aboyne legend. It was at once seen that the first line *Aboyne.* read—

MAQQOITALLUORRH,
Maqqoi talluorrh,

where the *h* has evidently the same force as in the "Ingeborh" of the Stennis Runes, and, no one doubts, makes up the name of a Pictish Talorg. The second line remained unread till Mr. Skene, our Celto-Scottish historian, detected in it what seems the Ogham equivalents of an expression in use in old Picto-Scottish charters. The Book of the Monastery of Deer, in recording the grants made to that community by the kings and nobles of Pictland, uses two forms of expression— *do rat*, "donavit," and *ro bait*, "immolavit." The reason for the distinction may now, perhaps, be apparent. Grants to the Celtic church were made, as well through voluntary piety as in condonation of personal immoralities. Those recorded in the Welsh Book of Llandaff were almost all made by transgressors of the moral or ecclesiastical law, in consideration of re-admission to church privileges. If *do rat* be proper to voluntary grants, and *ro bait* to these compulsory ones, we would understand the reason for something peculiar in the Ogham now under consideration. Mr. Skene renders it—

$$\widetilde{\text{NEAHH}}\,{}_{\text{HGL}}^{\text{T F}}\text{AROBBSDOCE}\overset{\text{? CC}\sim}{\underset{\text{TC}}{\text{ANNEFF.}}}$$

Neahhtla robbait Ceanneff.

"Neahhtla" (which he regards as a form of Nechtan) granted (immolavit) Kenneff," a known place-name in the district of the Mearns. The grantor's name, if it be Neachtan, is presented under a singularly ambiguous and confusing form. It may be read *Neahhtla, Neahhhgla, Neahhhola, Neahhhof, Neahhhong*, according as some of the digits are taken as crossing or stopping short at the medial line. They show on both sides, but so slightly on one that it might be doubted whether these sources of confusion arise from carelessness or design. If *Robbait*, however, imports that this is the name of one whose donation was an enforced mulct for an ecclesiastical offence, we see the relevancy of MacCurtin's statement about the evil actions of the dead being engraved on their monuments in forms of Ogham illegible to the uninitiated, and may be satisfied to conclude that probably none of the above various readings expresses the real name of the delinquent who, we have supposed, mortified Kenneff for his transgressions. It is to be observed that in extracting *robbait* from the text, the force of *ai* is given to the siglum, which has been elsewhere taken for *s*, slightly varied, and on the authority only of the exigence of the context.

217. The other Fifeshire Ogham monument, at Scoonie, offers an animated representation of a stag-hunt. The Ogham is carried up at one side ; and must be deemed to have been engraved after the sculpturing of the chase, as one limb of the stag projects across its digit-band, and that has a corresponding discontinuance.   The mysterious elephant-like symbol, often Scotland appearing on the Scottish sculptured stones, surmounts the scene.   Its presence might alone assure us that the hunt is typical and has an inner meaning.   Other grounds, however, exist for the same conclusion.   The subject is one of very frequent occurrence, both in ecclesiastical lapidary sculpture and wood-carving.   The sculptured slab of the stone coffin of St. Andrew's gives, I imagine, a key to the emblematical character of them all.   Here, at one side is the substituted ram of the sacrifice of Abraham.   At the other, a mounted hunter pursues the deer, which is entangled in the thicket.   A footman below chases wild beasts, which seem to elude him.   A composite creature, half-lion half-eagle, of frequent occurrence in church sculpture, preys on a carcass in the foreground at the feet of a Samson rending the jaws of the lion, all intensely Christian, recondite, and symbolical. It is enough for the present purpose to point out that the object of the horseman's chase is not the typical ram, but its antitype, so that if we accept the analogy of the St. Andrew's monument, these hunting scenes point to the pursuit of salvation in Christ.   The picture, however, has a reverse, in which I would suppose the theme of the Wild Huntsman has its origin. The most notable illustration known to me is that on the portal of St. Zeno's at Verona, where a mounted king pursues a stag with horn and hounds, but his horse has been provided by Satan, and bears him to the infernal gates.   There is a vague idea, which I have not traced to any certain source, that it represents Theodoric carried to destruction by heresy.   The accompanying Latin legend countenances the interpretation—

O Regem stultum : petit infernale tributum,
Moxque paratur equus quem misit demon iniquus,
Exit aquila nisus petit infera non rediturus.
Nisus equus ferus canis.
His datur hos dat averno.

Oh, the mad King, he seeks his doleful dues
On steed the devil finds him for his use,
Hawk, eagle, horse, hound, bounding beast, to these
He's given ; these gives he for perdition's fees.

His fatal quarry, so, with hound and horn,
He hunts through Hell-gate, never to return.

What the eagle or eagle-hawk may mean in either composition I do not attempt to explain, but infer that the hunt on the Scoonie standing stone is, like that on the St. Andrew's stone coffin slab, allegorical, and that, as regards the horses of the riders it is in contrast with that at St. Zeno's. The Ogham expresses but a single name which seems to me to be—

EDDARRNONN.
Eddarrnonn.

Whether the Ettern and Edeyrn of British examples in the diminutive, like Adamnan, or Eddarnon like the Irish Edarscal, I do not take on me to pronounce. The name of

Eddarrnonn is found also on the Brodie Stone in Elginshire. The same name in the modified form of *Iturnan* and *Ithurnan* occurs in the Irish annals at the years 665 and 669 in connection with Pictland. A further proof is afforded by the fact that traces of the ordinary sign of filiation are found in the inscription itself next after the characters in question. There is, first, a *lacuna* affording room for *m* and a vowel, followed by *qi*. But, unless this *i* be treated as an "iterate" or else be appropriated to the beginning of a succeeding vocable, nothing intelligible, so far as I can see, will emerge from the remaining groups. Accepting the *q*, however, as terminating *miq* or *meq*, the *i* will ally itself with what follows in a not unlikely sequence, disclosing something which, in this view, would appear to be a Pictish *matronymic*—

$$\text{EDDARRNONNmeQINGe}N\overset{\widetilde{\ \ }}{}\underset{GG}{R}\text{RuN}\overset{URB}{\underset{\underset{\underset{\&c.}{STF}}{EEL}}{}}\text{URH},$$

or, dividing the words, and accepting the forces for the uncertain characters most agreeable to their contexts—

Eddarrnonn meq ingen Rrunurborh,

that is, Eddarnon son of the daughter [lady] Runurborh. Eddarnon must be deemed a personage of note to have had his name inscribed on two out of the six Ogham monuments of Pictland, and, from the fact of both bearing symbolical SCOTLAND. sculpture, may be well supposed to have been an ecclesiastic. The legend appears to be continued on the opposite edge of the slab. Here, also, the characters are much confused by weather erosions, and present many perplexing alternatives—

$$\mathrm{ST}^{\,E}_{\&c.}{}^{G}_{O}\mathrm{NNMAQQDIMA}^{\;U}_{AC}{}^{G}\mathrm{C}_{T}\mathrm{OLL}^{U}_{O}\mathrm{MB}^{A}_{O}{}^{N}_{S}[$$

But for the apparent *tt* preceding $oll^{u}_{o}mban$, there would be no question that the *Eddarnon* of the monument is here brought into contact with a *Columbanus*; and there is no doubt that the *Colman* or *Columbanus* of the Paschal controversy, A.D. 664, was the contemporary of the *Ithurnan* of the annals. Our judgment in this difficulty may be legitimately influenced by the consideration that the division of the questionable digits into groups of two and four, instead of three and three, appears necessary to complete not only the initial of the name which follows, but also the termination of the word which precedes, viz., *Egnnuqqdig*; and this, if it be assimilable to its seeming Celtic equivalent *Ecnecdach*, must have an ending corresponding to *dach*, of which *d* and *i* are already ascertained. "*Ecnecdach*" may be rendered "antagonist," "expulsor." If it is rightly supposed to be represented by the barbaric *Egnnuqqdig* of the inscription, it is plain that Eddarrnonn is here shown in relations of antagonism to some Columbanus, importing one date for both. But the Columbanus of contentious repute in Scottish history is he of Lindisfarne, whence we may infer with some measure of assurance that the *Ithurnan* and *Columbanus* of the Annals are none other than the *Eddarnan* and *Columban* of the Brodie monument.

A second set of Oghams formerly existed on the cross-signed face of the Brodie stone. The only portion of these now in any degree legible is on the lower right-hand margin. It has a definite termination at top. Read from below upward, it yields nothing pronounceable. Read downward normally, it yields vocables commencing *osf*, suggesting some such proper name as Osfric, but complicated by what seems a *t* after *f*. Read downward from the opposite side, the characters yield an equally unpronounceable but also Anglo-Saxon-like name, followed by what looks very like a designation of nationality—

$$\text{OCTFR}_{S\,F}^{\,L}\text{ANGLA.}$$
$$S$$

In whatever way it may be regarded, the Anglo-Saxon element seems to be present, and lends additional force to the considerations which have already associated these Scottish memorials with reminiscences of the Council of Whitby.

Whatever is known in British history respecting the Council of Whitby is derived from the third Book of Beda. From his statements it may be collected that in the time of Finan, the successor of Aidan and predecessor of Colman in the See of Lindisfarne, questions had been raised respecting the Columban or northern Irish paschal practice by Ronan, a southern Irish monk. Colman, who had been deputed from Iona to preach to the English, succeeding Finan, found himself exposed to the same charges of heterodoxy by other assailants, led by Wilfrid, the domestic chaplain of King Oswy, and tutor of his son Alchfrid. To settle these disputes, Oswy convened both parties at the monastic house of St. Hilda, and, on debate of the matter, gave judgment against Colman. Thereupon Colman, " finding his doctrine repudiated and his sect contemned," set sail from Lindisfarne, taking with him the remnant of the Irish there, as well as thirty English adherents, and some relics also of Saint Aidan, and proceeded by way of Iona to Inisbofin, on the west coast of Ireland, whence, owing to differences among his followers, he withdrew with his English disciples to the mainland, where he founded the monastery of Mayo for them and their countrymen, and afterwards retiring to the " insula vaccæ albæ," died there, as we learn from the Annals of Ulster, which throughout call him Columbanus, A.D. 675. Beda, who names some of the synodical assembly, has no mention of any Iturnan, but names an Agatho who came on the part of Wilfrid. The withdrawal of Colman may well have been regarded as an expulsion by those of the opposite party ; and if we now find an Eddarnon of Anglo-Saxon associations commemorated as one of his expellers, there will be nothing repugnant to the historical facts hitherto known to us. The notice of Iturnan's and another's death in the annals— "Iturnan [Ithurnan] et Corinda [Corendu, Corenda] apud Pictones [Pictons] defuncti sunt"—may perhaps indicate that their parts in public affairs entitling them to historic mention had been played elsewhere than in Pictland. However this may be, it cannot be doubted that a memorial of anyone concerned against Colman in the Paschal controversy, A.D. 664, bearing the symbols peculiar to the sculptured stones of Pictland, would give rise to considerations of very great historical interest. For, a century from the time of the Pictish conversion by Columba must appear a surprisingly short time for the growth, not only of a non-Columban system of religious symbols, but of an anti-Columban ecclesiasticism, if these were not survivals of some form of pre-Columban Christianity in Pictland.

218. The mystical chase, however, is but one of a great number of lapidary devices of an extraordinary kind which occur as well on Ogham as on other stone monuments throughout the old Pictish part of Scotland. Some of them have been incidentally referred to, but any attempt to read inscriptions so accompanied would be imperfect without a more extended notice of them; and therefore, though I do not expect to bend the bow of Ulysses so as to send the arrow through all the rings, I shall endeavour to some extent to place before you the material for forming an opinion as to the meaning of these singular objects.

219. Dr. Joseph Anderson, of Edinburgh, has the distinction of having demonstrated the Christian character of several of these monuments independently of the crosses engraved on them. A cross, indeed, does not absolutely and of necessary inference show a monument to be Christian. There are, no doubt, Pagan crosses of various forms, from the Filfot or Swastica found by Schliemann on objects of old Trojan ware, to the Greek rectangular cross of equal arms found under the boundary mounds of the Roman agrimensores. But the general presumption in favour of the Christian symbol being

L

of Christian times is so strong, that one cannot but think those antiquaries over fastidious who decline to accept its evidence on the monuments of an ancient Christian country, because it is accompanied by unexplained forms of animals and other devices of crescent moons, circles, and sceptres, with which Dr. Stuart in his magnificent work has made the learned world familiar.

220. These objects accompany the cross on several monuments of this class, which Dr. Anderson has demonstrated to be Christian by comparing one of their sculptured features with the Jonah and Whale of the Catacombs, and of mediæval metal work. He has also identified other objects on the same monuments with what may be called scenes in Natural History, drawn from a peculiar kind of literature which still, I believe, rests in MS., in the Bestiaries of the later middle ages. The Bestiaries are compendiums of such knowledge in zoology and other branches of biological science as was current among the educated classes from the early Christian times down to the fifteenth and sixteenth centuries. It was a kind of reading aiming at entertainment and piety as well as instruction. Many of the creatures described and pictured are fabulous and chimerical in form; and many of the stories told of the non-fabulous ones are more designed for doctrinal and moral than scientific application. The lioness brings forth her cubs dead, till the lion, on the third day, breathes on them and so calls them to life. The tigress, when the hunter has stolen her cub, is stopped in her pursuit of him by a glass ball which he throws in her path, and in which seeing her own diminished image, she fancies she has her cub again, and stops to fondle it till the hunter makes his escape. Both these scenes Dr. Anderson has strong ground for claiming to have found on Scottish sculptured monuments of the class in question; and has, so far, advanced the growing proof of their Christian and not very ancient character.

221. I propose to carry the proofs farther, and to place before you some evidences on which, I do not doubt, you will conclude the entirely Christian nature of all these objects, and possibly the particular significance of some of them. I shall begin with the animal figures, and, with Dr. Anderson, take my first examples from the Catacombs. Here, we readily recognise our Lord in the Good Shepherd, and the Piping Shepherd. Equally obvious is the symbolism of our Lord in the character of Orpheus taming the rude nature of man by the harmonies of the divine message. From the classically-attired Orpheus of the tomb of St. Calixtus, with his seven-stringed lyre and attendant audience of the beasts of the field, to the unclothed human figure which is next presented from the western façade of the Cathedral of Ferrara, playing on his violin, there is a wide diversity in taste and in reverentness of technical treatment and expression, but not in meaning, as is evidenced by the animal attendants and their attitudes of submission and pleasure. I might cite other examples, especially those figures of the Piping Shepherd, and the Orpheus on the great cross of Clonmacnois, but, for the deeper symbolisms of the Scottish sculptures, it is necessary to go several steps farther. The figures, so far, are human, but we must be prepared to look without astonishment on other forms of the same idea. On the pulpit of San Ambrogio's, at Milan, a tenth-century work, are seen among other highly mystical devices, representations of a lion and a lamb respectively playing on triangular harps, with their several animal attendants. Were the analogies to stop here, there would be little hesitation in recognising the Lion of the tribe of Judah, and the Lamb that takes away the sin of the world, engaged in the same Orphic reformation of the brutish element in our nature. But the allegory is carried on through further disguises, partly mere animal; such as the bear which plays on the Celtic harp over one of the transept windows at Chartres, with other forms still more derogatory to the subject in manuscript and printed books; and partly composite—animal and human,—of which latter class is the Centaur from the porch of the Cathedral of St. Zeno, at Verona, playing on a square lyre and accompanied by the usual attendant. The next example, even more instructive for the purposes of our immediate inquiry, taken from the exterior of the south transept of the Cathedral of Genoa, shows an equine figure playing the same part in precisely a similar scene, but with some differences worthy of closer notice. The side of the creature is rent, as are the sides of the victims which may be seen in the paws of the lions at most of the cathedral doorways in North Italy, and its fore feet, with which it touches the strings of the instrument, are not solidungular but divided. An example of the same heterogeneous mixture of animal varieties may be seen in an Agnus Dei of so late a date as the sixteenth century in the cloister of the University of Pavia. It is ovine in all its traits, save its leonine tail and clawed feet. The tail, indeed, in all these mystical animal forms is conventionalised, and gives notice that something esoteric and Christian is hidden under the barbarous outlines.

222. The digital feet unite these latter examples with other symbolisms carrying us another step nearer the Scottish sculptures, through a connection for which it is necessary to resort to the early Christian monuments of Scandinavia. Here also are found digital-footed equine figures whose outlines, treated in a manner peculiar, so far as I know, to Norse and Picto-Scottish monuments, show a general relation between the schools of sculpture and a resemblance almost amounting to identity between part of the Norse composition and one of the more peculiar Scottish emblems. The figures referred to are found at three several localities in Sweden, and may be seen engraved in Stephens's "Runic Monuments." Their singularities consist, first, in curved prolongations of the upper outlines of the limbs, producing spirals and volutes over the body. These spirals are found similarly situated on the symbolic animals forming the interlaced ornamentation of the Moneymusk reliquary, and are familiar to our eyes in great numbers of the Scottish and Irish lapidary sculptures. I would, next, instance the re-entrant and divergent curves of the outlines, quite in the manner of what is known as the Celtic trumpet pattern. This pattern pervades Celtic ecclesiastical decorative work, and is conspicuous on some examples of what is known as the 'envelope' object on the Scottish inscribed stones. Of its ecclesiastical use I would suppose there can be no doubt, and that most probably it is meant for a satchel or book-cover. Let us now observe the curled and convoluted outlines of the

head and jaws, and compare these with the curled and floriated outlines of the Norrie's Law symbol, as seen in its conventionalised reproductions on the Scottish incised stones.
It must be owned that the latter bears an extraordinary likeness to the neck and head of the Swedish symbol. Why a
portion only of the figure should be adopted into the Scottish
emblematical technology, I am in no position to explain, but
a glance into that storehouse of mystical learning lately produced by the Benedictines at Solesme, in Normandy, the
"Spicilegium Solesmense," serves to show the mediæval idea
underlying the entire equine series. At No. 767 of Theodulf's
Recensio of the Clavis of Melito (a species of concordance to
the figurative language of Scripture) is the entry, "Equus,
corpus Domini," so that it may be predicated with considerable
confidence of this floriated Norrie's Law object on the
Scottish sculptures that it is Christian, symbolical, and
eucharistic.

223. In one of the Scottish figures, that of the elephant,
the terminal convolutions, which in the Swedish symbolic
creature are confined to the face and jaw, are extended to all
the extremities. The Clavis ascribes no special meaning to
the elephant; but in the Bestiaries it is treated as the emblem of
Chastity. Whether it be a type merely of a particular virtue,
and so referable to the Mother of our Lord, or be a symbol
having a more universal meaning, this device of the trans-
figurated elephant has associations apparently carrying back
its use in Scotland, where alone it has been found, into the
age of urn-burial and of the use of bronze weapons. It is
engraved on a stone said to have been found above the
covering-stone of a kist which enclosed an urn and bronze
dagger, at Carngrig, Forfarshire. (Proc. Soc. Antiq. Scot.,
15th Feb., 1865.) It has also been found among works
presumably of the Roman period. That it was always of
Christian import, I myself am strongly persuaded; and if it
be so, it carries back Christianity in Scotland to a surprisingly
early date, and tends powerfully to set up the old traditions
of Boece and Fordun. Its curled extremities show that the
taste which has disguised the outline of the Swedish symbolic
equine figures in similar convolutions was of vastly older

prevalence in North Britain, and goes almost the whole way
in displacing the idea that the Scoto-Pictish carvings are of
Scandinavian origin. How, then, it will be said, can this be
deemed a ninth or tenth century symbol in those monuments
where we have found it accompanied by Oghams seemingly
of so late a period? The answer must be found in the
persistence of types, and I would imagine the nursery of the
type must be looked for in Byzantine symbolography.

224. In this connexion, let me observe that an earlier
Christianity than that usually accorded to the Picts is strongly
argued by the language of St. Patrick in his epistle to
Coroticus, where he reproaches the Picts with having become
apostate while a Roman municipal and military establishment
still subsisted at Strathclyde, which could hardly have been
after A.D. 410, when the Romans took their final departure
from Britain. It is true this would put the date of Patrick,
the son of Calphurn, before the mission of Palladius; but
many arguments for that position may be drawn from the
documents preserved in the Book of Armagh and from the
Coroticus Epistle. Not the least cogent of these, in my mind,
is the absence from Patrick's authentic writings of any reference to a predecessor in the missionary field, while his statement that in the scene of his own labours the want that had
been experienced was a want of regular ministers of religion,
implies that there were already everywhere believers to be
served.

225. I shall now seek the meaning of another animal form
of occasional occurrence on the Scottish monuments, in what
must always be the chief source of knowledge in Christian
symbolism—the objects themselves seen in actual ecclesiastical
sculpture. It is the seemingly canine creature found notably
on the Bressay and Golspie stones, and also conspicuous on
the decorated cross at Drumcliffe in Ireland. On the western
portal of St. Apollinaris at Trent, but not of an antiquity
equalling that of the building, is a boldly-executed figure of
a composite creature, in which we do not hesitate to
recognise Him of whom it is said, " Thou shalt tread upon
the lion and adder: the young lion and the dragon shalt
thou trample under feet." The cherubic disguise at St.

Apollinaris, is exchanged for another presentation of the same Scotland. Being at the porch of St. Bolzen, where the walker on the dragon is figured in the canine form. Under the same derogatory disguise the same allegory occurs again at the eastern door of Trent Cathedral. We are shocked at the irreverence of this kind of religion, but compelled to give it the meaning which Scripture supplies. Three of these creatures appear on the Bressay monument, one single, and on the opposite side two breathing as it were into one another's open jaws, and, between them, exhaling a something represented by a circular disk.

226. Not pausing here to speculate on the meaning, further than to say that the associated figures show it, if significant, to be symbolical and Christian, I may now approach the consideration of the Golspie monument, where *Golspie.* the canine creature occurs in company not only with most of the peculiar emblematic devices of Picto-Scottish sculpture, but with a human figure engaged in significant action in relation to it. At top the monument presents the object known as the envelope; below it the elephant; below these, at one side, the human figure; at the other, three objects, namely, this canine creature voluted like the Scandinavian Norse emblems; below it the emblematic fish; below the fish the object I have designated the Norrie's Law symbol. In a triad of emblems, the central one of which is the ἰχθύς, we may without irreverence perceive the relative meanings of the other two. Against this triad a human figure armed with an axe in one hand and a knife in other, is shown advancing in an attitude of attack. The dress is secular and the aspect hostile. We turn to the Ogham context in the legitimate hope that it may throw some light on the scene. If it have any relevancy, and be at all decipherable, it ought to inform us of some action affecting some mystery of the Christian religion. It occupies the edge of the stone, and, at the commencement especially, is a highly artificialised example of Ogham writing. The edge of the flag is rounded, and without any medial line. It is left doubtful whether some of the digits are intended to cross the whole field of the edge-surface, or to be confined to one side of the suppressed *medium filum.*

Further difficulty arises from the contrariety of slope given to digits seemingly belonging to the same categories. But when, undeterred by these confusions, one applies the ordinary key to the digits according to their position over, under, or across the central part of the field, accepting the vertical digits as vocalic, some Celtic words do indeed seem to shape themselves out of these elements having a real relation to the sculptured subject. One of these appears to be intended for *aiffroin*, the Mass. This adaptation of the *offerendum* or *oblatio* of the Latins is the universal insular Celtic equivalent for the eucharistic offering. If it be here intended, it is presented in the form *aiffhrrenn*. The word, at its commencement, is defined by a point separating it from the immediately preceding vocables. These appear to express *ac a tan*, "at his *tan*." *Tan*, that is, "plunder," "plundering expedition," a "driving," or "raid," as in the *Tain bo Cuailnge*, the *Tain bo Dartada*, &c. Who, then, is he whom we have these reasons to regard as being thus shown at his Mass raid? It certainly gives renewed corroboration to MacCurtin's statement about writing the evil deeds of men in difficult Oghams on their monuments that almost all the devices for obscuring this legend are employed in the earlier part of it, containing the name which should answer that question. It begins with the character to which, in the Lunnasting example, we have ascribed the power of *s*, and it ends with *eadda*; but further I am unable to lift the veil, unless I were to resort to assumptions and conjectures for which I am not at present prepared. Still it will admit of question, even supposing that I have rightly interpreted both symbols and legend, whether the commemoration is condemnatory. It was one of the pedantries of Irish ecclesiastical writers to "use the technical language of plundering for the expression of religious sentiment" (Stokes, Fel., Feb. 17th, Miscel. Celt. Soc., 338), and one of the few passages in which the author of the Félire rises into imaginative exaltation is that at May 17th, in which he treats three saints "as if they were three Irish chieftains making a raid in their war-chariots into heaven" (*ib.*). He celebrates—

"The hosting (sluagad) of Adrio, of Victor, of Basil: they unyoked without a whit of weakness on a height of Heaven's Kingdom."

So here the knife and hatchet may but signify the urgency and frequency of the oblation by a worshipper bent on winning heaven by assault.   But, had this been the true meaning, less pains would probably have been taken in disguising the name of the offerer.

227. The remaining objects comprise two which occur very frequently and conspicuously on these Picto-Scottish monuments.   Below the triad, the sceptre-traversed crescent, and the object known as the "spectacle ornament."   If we apply the rule *noscitur a sociis*, we must infer them to be symbolical and Christian; and from what has been seen of the tri-radial device in Welsh symbolism, we may incline to allow that the tri-sceptral one of the Scottish monuments has also relation to the same mystery of the Godhead.   This symbol in a bi-sceptral form traverses the crescent; in a tri-sceptral form, the other emblem, whatever it may signify.   I imagine the meaning of both may be inferred from the symbolic interpretation of *luna* in the *Clavis*, "Luna, Maria Virgo" ("Spicileg.," vol. ii., p. 66), because of her increase in the Incarnation.   It is difficult with due reverence to treat this subject in words as fully as our forefathers have treated it in their carved emblems.   Many of those, especially in Ireland, are greatly coarser in their methods of expression than these Scottish examples, but all of them appear to relate to that human condition to which our Lord condescended when He took upon Him to deliver man.

228. Looking back, now, on the entire subject, there appear to be two questions of primary importance for the historian and philologist : Is this method of writing, of Pagan or of Christian origin ? and, Is the language in which these names and formulas are expressed a *quasi* hieratic dialect, not trammelled by the ordinary laws of Celtic speech, or is it the vernacular language of those who carved the inscriptions ?   No treatment of the first question is likely to be satisfactory which does not fully investigate that class of *quasi* Oghams and *pseudo* Oghams of which I have spoken as abounding in the South of Ireland, as well as all the remains of inscriptional figuring on the Pagan sepulchral monuments of the Boyne and Slieve-na-Calliagh districts.   As regards the second, I am content to leave it in the hands of those who have made the philosophy of language their study, claiming only the credit of having supplied their researches with approximately authentic *data* in the texts I have presented.

INDEX TO OGHAM LEGENDS.

CHAPTER VII.

INDEX.

PETER ROE, PRINTER, MABBOT-STREET, DUBLIN.

BIBLIOLIFE

Old Books Deserve a New Life
www.bibliolife.com

Did you know that you can get most of our titles in our trademark **EasyScript**™ print format? **EasyScript**™ provides readers with a larger than average typeface, for a reading experience that's easier on the eyes.

Did you know that we have an ever-growing collection of books in many languages?

Order online:
www.bibliolife.com/store

Or to exclusively browse our **EasyScript**™ collection:
www.bibliogrande.com

At BiblioLife, we aim to make knowledge more accessible by making thousands of titles available to you – quickly and affordably.

Contact us:
BiblioLife
PO Box 21206
Charleston, SC 29413

9702528R0010